Happily Ever After

17

Happily Ever After

*Fairy Tales, Children,
and the Culture Industry*

Jack Zipes

Routledge
New York and London

Published in 1997 by

Routledge
29 West 35th Street
New York, NY 10001

Published in Great Britain in 1997 by

Routledge
11 New Fetter Lane
London EC4P 4EE

Copyright © 1997 by Routledge

Printed in the United States of America
Design: Jack Donner

Library of Congress Cataloging-in-Publication Data

Zipes, Jack David.
Happily ever after : fairy tales, children, and the culture industry / by Jack Zipes
p.   cm.
Includes bibliographical references and index.
ISBN 0–415–91850–2 (cloth). — ISBN 0–415–91851–0 (pbk.)
1. Fairy tales—History and criticism.   2. Folklore and children—History and criticism.
3. Fairy tales—Film and video adaptations.   4. Discourse analysis, Narrative.   I. Title.
GR550.Z58   1997
398.2—dc20   96–38237
CIP

To Thomas Hoernigk,
good friend and mensch

Contents

Acknowledgments

For the past three years I have been exploring the interconnections between the oral folk tale, the literary fairy tale, and the fairy tale as film, and many of the essays in this book stem from talks that I delivered on this topic in England, Ireland, and the United States during this period. Two of the chapters were first published in *The Lion and the Unicorn* and *In Front of the Children: Screen Entertainment and Young Audiences*. They have both been completely revised and expanded for this book.

As I worked on these essays, I benefited a great deal from the suggestions and critical advice of Cary Bazalgette, Nancy Canepa, and Catherine Vellay-Vallantin. In addition, Marina Warner and Rüdiger Steinlein have been especially helpful in elucidating complex issues in the historical development of the fairy tale. As usual, I have relied on Bill Germano and Christine Cipriani for their sound advice and guidance, and I have profited greatly from the careful copyediting of Connie Oehring.

The present study was not conceived as a book, and yet the essays were written to address my ongoing interrelated concerns about the socialization of children, the impact of the fairy tale on children and adults, and the future development of the fairy tale as film. At the same time, my interest in storytelling has increased, and I have sought to explore the renascence of storytelling in general and its relationship to the culture industry's effect on story. As a result of analyzing the historical trajectory of storytelling and the literary fairy tale, the essays in this book move from the sixteenth century to the present, between different cultures and societies, and from specific analyses to general syntheses that are often somewhat provocative and speculative. In the end, I hope that the common threads of my arguments are woven carefully enough to clarify why I believe that fairy tales in all their forms have such profound meaning in our pursuit of happiness.

Introduction

No social scientist need prove a direct effect on children's behavior for some of us to hate the bullying, conformist shabbiness of the worst pop and the way it consumes our children. If children are living in pop culture, and a good part of it is ugly and stupid, that is effect enough; the sheer cruddiness is an affront.

—David Denby

As children, we all hear fairy tales and read our lives into them. But we also want to see and realize our lives as virtual fairy tales even as we grow older. We never abandon fairy tales. So it is not by chance that the fairy-tale film has become the most popular cultural commodity in America, if not the world. In recent years such films as *Beauty and the Beast*, *Never Ending Story II*, *The Lion King*, and *Aladdin* have earned millions of dollars and entertained millions of viewers, not to mention the re-releases of such classics as *Snow White and the Seven Dwarfs*, *Sleeping Beauty*, and *Pinocchio* and the hundreds of fairy-tale films made for the video market, such as *The Return of Jafar* and *Aladdin and the King of Thieves*, and fairy-tale films produced for television, the most prominent being Ron Koslow's 1986 series *Beauty and the Beast*. If we include live-action films such as *Splash*, *The Princess Bride*, *Pretty Woman*, *Into the West*, and the hundreds of sentimental films that rely on the fairy-tale structure in which a magical transformation or miraculous event brings about a satisfying, happy ending, we could possibly argue that Hollywood itself as an industry and a trademark is inseparable from the fairy tale. In fact, Hollywood as a symbol is a utopian fairy-tale destination, a place where the good fairy as destiny waits to transform unknown talents into known stars, where fortunes are made, where, like the enchanted forest, something special happens that brings genuine happiness to the true in heart.

But Hollywood—like other centers of the entertainment industry in the United States and Europe—is also a hard and cruel place. The people who first built up Hollywood always knew it, and everyone who works in entertainment in Hollywood today knows it too. Like the Wizard of Oz, Hollywood "producers" rely on illusion to impress audiences and to maintain the fiction of Hollywood as utopia. Perhaps this is one reason that filmmakers were attracted to the genre of the fairy tale from the very beginning. Knowing full well that they could not provide happiness in or through their films, they needed true and tested stories to continue framing and narrating the wish-fulfillments of all classes of people to give them hope—and, of course, to make some money in the process.

It would be simplistic, however, to attribute the adaptation of folk tales and fairy tales to the screen to the materialist interests of early-twentieth-century filmmakers. If anything, these filmmakers were more enthralled by the dazzling technology of making films, whether animated or live-action. Certainly they also wanted success and fame, and many of their own lives read like Horatio Alger stories that are not unlike fairy tales. But just as important as notoriety and money was the challenge of resolving technical and aesthetic problems in producing films so that the images on the screen would be more effective in creating the illusion of possibility and actuality. Early filmmakers took great joy and pride in the discovery of the appropriate forms, shapes, movements, and constructions that would best give expression to the genius of their invention. Fairy tales were incidental to their work. Filmmakers did not realize how rich and compelling fairy-tale material really was until the 1930s—coincidentally, just as the great economic Depression was shaking most of the world and causing widespread misery; just as fascism of all kinds was on the rise. The fairy tale was to speak for happiness and utopia in the face of conditions that were devastating people's lives all over the globe. Perhaps this utopian message was why Disney's *Snow White and the Seven Dwarfs* was such a great success in 1937.

Yet the fairy tale was not used consciously in the 1930s to provide an opiate for the people. Cinematic adaptation and transformation of the literary fairy tale was a gradual process that began in the 1890s with the innovative experiments of Georges Méliès and continues today with many significant ramifications and a range of complex meanings. Few critics have bothered to explore how the rise of the cinema affected the fairy-tale genre and how the function of the fairy tale as a literary genre shifted and was altered with the rise of the fairy-tale film and the development of the culture industry from the late 1920s to the present.

To write about the historical transformations of the fairy tale means writing about struggles over voice, storytelling, and the socialization of children. If, in fact, the fairy tale emanated from an oral tradition in which small groups of people interacted with a storyteller, generally a member of the group, who responded to their needs and demands, then this narrative form, while not "pure" folk art, did have immediate significance for the teller and hearers, representing their belief systems and tastes in a voice or voices with which they identified. Such tales were never owned or copyrighted, though it was easy for members of particular groups or communities to recognize the "properties" of a specific tale—to call it their own. As an oral form, the fairy tale was always one among many different oral genres; it was never categorized as a "children's" genre. Nor was it regarded as a genre for children when it was appropriated by educated upper-class writers in the sixteenth and seventeenth centuries in Italy and France. The literary fairy tales of Giovan Francesco Straparola, Giambattista Basile, Mme. D'Aulnoy, Charles Perrault, Mlle. L'Héritier, Mlle. de La Force, and others were complex symbolic social acts intended to reflect upon mores, norms, and habits organized for the purpose of reinforcing a hierarchically arranged civilizing process in a particular society. This formative civilizing character of the genre is also quite apparent in Shakespeare's fairy-tale plays such as *The Tempest* as well as in the operas and ballets of the seventeenth and eighteenth centuries. In other words, literary fairy tales appropriated oral folk tales and created new ones to reflect upon rituals, customs, habits, and ethics and simultaneously to serve as a civilizing agent. The fairy tale demonstrated what it meant to be beautiful and heroic and how to achieve "royal" status with the help of grace and good fortune. In addition, for many readers of that time, to read or listen to a fairy tale provided a means to distance themselves psychologically from their present situations and to be transported to a magical realm. To read a fairy tale was to follow the narrative path to happiness.

The literary voice was anonymous—and specific at the same time. Readers knew who the author was, but they did not know what the author represented or why he or she wrote the tale. They could not question the author as they could a live storyteller. The author of a literary fairy tale was mysterious, even as his or her work was becoming standardized and familiar. The works of fairy-tale writers became institutionalized during the eighteenth century, and audiences came to expect and demand certain kinds of structures, topoi, motifs, and characters in fairy tales as they formed a literary institution. Not all fairy tales were the same at the time that Jacob and Wilhelm Grimm, Hans Christian Andersen, Andrew Lang, and others made the fairy tale a popular genre in the nineteenth century. But they were all structured similarly to promise happiness if one could "properly" read their plots and symbols, even when tragedy occurred.

Proper reading, of course, became a key in the nineteenth century, and it was in the nineteenth century that the fairy tale experienced a split; it became schizoid. (Of course, we must keep in mind that the oral tradition was still alive and active and interacting with the literary tradition during this period.) Throughout the nineteenth century in Europe and North America, well-intentioned publishers, clergymen, educators, and parents began discussing "proper" reading material for children and setting criteria for stories that were considered beneficial. At first, fairy tales were regarded as dangerous because they lacked Christian teaching and their symbols were polymorphously meaningful and stimulating. But by the beginning of the nineteenth century, fairy-tale writers had learned to rationalize their tales and to incorporate Christian and patriarchal messages into the narratives to satisfy middle-class and aristocratic *adults*. For example, the Grimms purposely changed their fairy tales between 1819 and 1857 to make them more instructional and moral, and other writers worked to create tales more appropriate for children, not realizing that often, in seeking to protect children, we harm them most. Andersen, Wilhelm Hauff, Ludwig Bechstein, George Cruikshank, and Mme. Ségur are among the writers who sought to sweeten tales and to direct them at children in a wholesome fashion. At the same time, many writers during the latter half of the nineteenth century, such as George MacDonald, Lewis Carroll, and Oscar Wilde, used the fairy-tale-for-children form to question the overly didactic tales. The result in Western countries was the split and the commodification of the fairy tale. The split was complicated because the divide was not only between the literary fairy tale for adults and the wholesome tale for children, but also between "proper" and "improper" traits. One thing was clear—the "proper" fairy tale for children had become a hot commodity used expressly to socialize children in families and at schools.

Enter the radio and the film.

Both radio and film continued the literary tradition of separating the fairy tale for children from that for adults. However, it is quite clear that by the onset of the twentieth century, the fairy tale had become the predominant literary genre for middle-class children, especially preadolescent children, and it was also *family fare*. The entire family could read, listen, and view a fairy tale at the same time, and each member could "get something out of it." The crucial question in the early part of the twentieth century—one that is still pertinent—was how to package the tale to attract the largest audience: as book, radio program, or film. Once again, in radio and film the narrator's voice-over was both anonymous and specific. The voice was characteristically gentle, whether male or female, soft but assured, always promising that happiness would be achieved in the end. One need only listen to the voice in Disney's *Snow White and the Seven Dwarfs* or the CBS radio broadcasts of *Let's Pretend* with Nyla Mack during the 1940s. The voice-over is a governing voice, but it is not always needed, for the narrative itself carries an ordering voice, in dialogue, as we have learned from Bakhtin, with other voices.

There would seem to be something totalitarian about the manner in which the voice of the early oral fairy tales was stolen from real, live "people," appropriated through literature and used by corporations seeking to profit from our fantasies and longing for happiness. However, this kind of argument is facile and one-dimensional, emanating from a mechanical and deterministic view of human nature and history. Though there are certainly "totalitarian" aspects of the transformation of the fairy tale, it is more important to grasp the *diverse* ways in which the fairy tale as a genre has been used. The fairy tale has not only been conceived and exploited to manipulate children and adults, it has also been changed in innovative ways to instill hope in its youthful and mature audiences so that no matter now bad their lives are, they can still believe that they can live happily ever after.

The crucial question is how the culture industry compromises our notion of the pursuit of happiness gleaned from fairy tales. In what explicit and implicit ways must the culture be represented as ultimate authority and power, in much the same manner that Louis XIV, the Sun King, commanded his own representation in fairy tales written by Charles Perrault, Mme. D'Aulnoy, and others during the ancien régime? How did a specific rationalist aesthetics develop in the seventeenth century and make its way into the fairy-tale films of the twentieth-century culture industry?

In the twentieth century the creation of fairy tales in all their forms; their effective use by individual artists, corporations, and institutions; and their reception by different audiences take place within the culture industry. Simply put, all art, whether high or low, is subject to commodification, and this commodification has no other purpose than to capture and play upon—in order to profit from—our desire for pleasure and happiness. In order to maximize profit, the culture industry has to instill standard expectations in audiences so that they think they are getting what they want, and that by getting what they supposedly want, they can become like the stars with whom they identify. When accused of "dumbing down" their programs and products, corporate representatives in the culture industry are fond of announcing that they are conceding to the wishes of the public and are only as guilty as their audiences. Of course, they never mention that they seek to control these audiences through their own polls and conditioning processes. The culture industry is indeed "totalitarian"—perhaps one should use the word *global* today, given the globalization of corporate capitalism—in its intention to totally take over markets and dominate demands and wishes. Whether it completely succeeds is another question, and whether it "totally" infiltrates our lives is debatable. For David Denby, who has written a superb essay about this topic in the *New Yorker*, the situation for children is practically hopeless. "Sold a bill of goods from the time they are infants," he explains, "many of today's children, I suspect, will never develop the equipment to fight off the system of flattery and propitiation which soothes their insecurities and pumps their egos. By the time they are five or six, they've been pulled into the marketplace. They're on their way to becoming not citizens but consumers. It was not ever thus. Our reality has changed. The media have become three-dimensional, inescapable, omnivorous, and self-referring—a closed system that seems, for many of the kids, to answer all their questions."[1]

In contrast, it has become common among celebrators of popular culture such as John Fiske, Dominic Strinati, and many others to criticize Max Horkheimer and Theodor Adorno, the originators of the concept of a "culture industry," by pointing to the myriad ways in which common people make use of all kinds of commodities in guerrilla ways to liberate themselves and to develop subversive forms of culture that enable them to take control of their lives. Certainly there is some truth in what these critics say, but I fear that they exaggerate the "liberating" potential of commodified culture and the conscious autonomy of "the people," whoever they are supposed to be. Too often it seems to me that Fiske and other celebrators of popular culture fail to grasp how early the media penetrate the lives of children, how strong is the referential system of the culture industry, and how it sets the terms for socialization and education in the Western world. Cultural institutions in the twentieth century are centered around profit, power, and pleasure through power. It is how we learn about and make use of power strategies that gives us some sense of autonomy and pleasure. Popular culture is a myth because we cannot assume that what emanates from "the people" is theirs, that is, an expression of their authentic desires or wishes. These desires and wishes are not ours—even when we think they are or would like them to be—because we tend to forget what the culture industry does to our children and ourselves.

It is strange that in studies of popular culture, critics generally exclude children when they talk about "the people" who consume all sorts of cultural artifacts or make liberating use of them. Most studies of popular culture do not deal with children or with products expressly conceived and manufactured for children. Children are not popular in studies of popular culture, or in courses taught at the university. The intersections between so-called children's art and adult art are rarely studied. In fact, it is commonly known, despite substantial achievements in the field, that children's literature is given short shrift at the university as "kiddie lit," and it is hardly ever included in popular studies or cultural studies programs. It is as if the socialization of taste and the cultural artifacts of childhood have little or nothing to do with the manner in which we appreciate and make use of culture as adults. It is as though the games children play, the books they read, and the stories they tell have not already been influenced by the culture industry and will not play a role in their cultural lives as adults. Though great gains have been made at our universities in interdisciplinary studies, there is still a great deal of compartmentalization and specialization that narrow our perspective. And, of course, I am not talking only about the university.

In studying the fairy tale it is impossible to discuss the genre without opposing such compartmentalization; without investigating the intersections of oral, literary, audio, and electronic forms of the fairy tale; without examining the civilizing processes in different cultures, the formation of families, and the institutionalization of genres. But more to the point, especially in this book, it is crucial to grasp when and why children became the focus of fairy-tale writers and filmmakers and what role the fairy tale plays as literature, film, audiocassette, and electronic story in the lives of both children and adults. Though the traditional fairy tale has been greatly commodified, and though our lives appear to be continually governed by market demands and cost efficiency, new forms of fairy tales and storytelling have not been proscribed or prevented from emerging. Nor are we as subjects bound to be homogenized, our identities totally determined as types of commodities by the market demands and conditions of the culture industry. In fact, there have always been and still are many sites and signs of resistance inside the culture industry and on its margins.

Though I do not want to privilege the fairy tale as "cultural institution," it is uncanny how much we turn to this genre in all its forms to pursue our identities and the happy fulfillment of our goals, sometimes resisting and sometimes conforming to the rules of the culture industry. In this pursuit we use fairy tales as markers to determine where we are in our journey. The fairy tale becomes a broad arena for presenting and representing our wishes and desires. It frequently takes the form of a mammoth discourse in which we carry on struggles over family, sexuality, gender roles, rituals, values, and sociopolitical power. Writers stake out their ideological positions through fairy tales. For instance, such best-selling books as Robert Bly's *Iron John* (1990), Clarissa Pinkola Estés's *Women Who Run with the Wolves* (1993), and James Finn Garner's *Politically Correct Bedtime Stories* (1994) use the fairy tale to raise highly significant questions about social and political conditions, which reach broad audiences throughout the world. The authors, whose intentions vary a great deal, touch upon sensitive chords of the temper of our times, and their works are written and marketed to play upon the theme of the happiness that avoids us. Consequently, they have drawn remarkable responses in the form of parodies by other authors, such as Alfred Gingold's *Fire in the John: The Manly Man in the Age of Sissification* (1991) and Barbara Graham's *Women Who Run with the Poodles: Myths and Tips for Honoring Your Mood Swings* (1994) as well as serious essays in magazines and journals.

These writers of best-selling books are not the only ones to

channel their ideological views through fairy tales. In the past
three years alone, fifty or more fairy-tale books have been published in the United States which re-create traditional fairy tales
in order to address contemporary social problems. For example,
Robin McKinley's *Deerskin* (1993) is a fascinating psychological
exploration of Charles Perrault's "The Donkey-Skin"; Vivian
Vande Velde's *Tales from the Brothers Grimm and the Sisters Weird*
(1995) purports to "fracture" many of the Grimms' tales along the
same lines explored by Jim Henson in his Muppet films and
Edward Everett Horton in the television series *The Adventures of
Rocky and Bullwinkle*; Ellen Datlow and Terri Windling have edited
three significant anthologies, *Black Thorn, White Rose* (1993),
Snow White, Blood Red (1994), and *Ruby Slippers, Golden Tears*
(1995), which contain unusual contemporary versions of classical
tales by some of the most gifted fantasy and science fiction writers
in the United States; and Barbara Walker's *Feminist Fairy Tales*
(1996) is a collection of twenty-eight familiar folk and fairy tales
from an explicit feminist perspective with didactic overtones.
These books are for young and old readers. They are "crossover"
books, and if I were to focus on the other fairy-tale books published
specifically for children in the past five years, I would have to discuss a few hundred that either alter classical fairy tales according
to contemporary viewpoints as to what is proper for children or
create new fantastic stories that question the very notion of pro-
priety in language and behavior.

Even more appealing to children are fairy-tale films, which take
precedence over literature. I do not mean that children do not read
fairy tales anymore or have tales read to them. Rather, children are
more readily exposed to fairy-tale films through television and
movie theaters than through books—it is important to remember
that fairy-tale books are too expensive for most children to purchase, and if they read fairy-tale books at a young age, most will do
it at school or through a public library. Nonetheless, children are
continually exposed to fairy tales through reading, viewing, and
listening. They are encouraged to sort out their lives through fairy
tales, but too often they are served up the classical models of

Perrault, the Grimms, and Andersen or the contemporary equivalent in a Disney film that reinforces the patriarchal and consumer tendencies of the culture industry. Resistance to these models does not have to take the form of "politically correct" books, as I have tried to demonstrate in the anthology *The Outspoken Princess and the Gentle Knight* (1994), but rather occurs in tales that help young people question the familial and social standards that they are expected to respect and in tales that excite their imaginations and encourage them to explore their environments and to learn to make moral and ethical choices through involvement in challenging narratives.

Of course, storytelling through books and film is only one way that children can be induced to become their own decisionmakers and creators. Oral storytelling has never ceased, and it continues to play a significant role in our lives. Unfortunately, most university courses and studies of literature seem to imply that oral storytelling ended with the rise of the printing press, or that if it did not end, it has become insignificant in our lives. We know this idea to be untrue, but most university literature courses—except for courses on folklore—rarely take the connections between oral storytelling and literature into consideration. Obviously, the connections are extremely difficult to trace, and such investigation requires some training in anthropology, ethnology, and communication. Yet it is an important undertaking, especially given the renascence of storytelling in the Western world. Storytelling and fairy-tale associations such as the National Storytelling Association in the United States, the Society for Storytelling in the United Kingdom, or the Europäische Märchengesellschaft in Germany, to name but a few, have proliferated and, during the past fifteen to twenty years, have helped to develop an interest in storytelling in schools, theaters, libraries, hospitals, and old-age homes, as well as in therapy situations, with a focus on "recapturing" the live person-to-person storytelling relationship.

In my opinion this renascence is part of a reaction to the commodification of folk culture in a world of technology and is connected to folklore and folklorism. The renowned German folklorist Hermann Bausinger regards folklore as a counterworld because it implies a search for nature at a distance from conventionalized etiquette—it is connected to traditions that emanate from particular groups of people, are kept alive by these groups, and are not bound by convention. On the other hand, Bausinger maintains that folklorism "is a 'secondary, administered folk world,' ... it is effective because it has the semblance of the nonadministered, the original, the spontaneous, the naturally evolved."[2] Examples of folklorism are the imitation of folklore for commercial purposes; the creation of fictitious rituals through the making, wearing, and selling of "peasant," primitive, or ethnic artifacts, costumes, jewelry, furniture, and so on; the re-creation of folk rituals through dancing, song, and music that are put on display and are alleged to represent the "true" spirit of a particular ethnic group; the return to indigenous crafts as a hobby, such as the making of quilts, furniture, and costumes. In the case of storytelling, folklorism can be identified in storytellers who dress up in "native" costumes or assume the guise of an authentic shaman or wise person and endeavor to re-create the "genuine" tone and ritual of a storyteller of the past. Obviously there is something escapist and phony in such a retreat to the past. But Bausinger poses an important question here:

> Are there not attempts at humanizing, at a new self-determination and spontaneity, contained in the retreat to forms of former folk culture which are often preindustrial in origin and structure? This question should not be simply ignored. It definitely renders an essential motif of folklorism tangible—the need to escape from a world that has become extremely unintelligible and unwieldy into a realm that is intelligible, manageable, and familiar. But here, too, appearances are deceptive when it comes to the fulfillment of such needs. What appears as an enclave of the authentic (relative to objects this again means as a relic) is in reality most often contrived, organized, prepared, and at the very least "cultivated."[3]

In each country of the Western world the resurgence of storytelling is manifesting itself in different ways that reflect the currents of folklorism and folklore. In the United States, for instance, many ethnic minority groups are endeavoring to use storytelling to recover their history and to keep rituals alive in a dynamic way. Storytellers create family sagas out of their personal experiences, research different types of tales and retell them in highly dramatic ways, put on performances for children in schools. There are storytelling festivals, workshops, classes, and demonstrations. There are professional and amateur storytellers, and there are people who know how to weave great stories without even realizing that they are relating certain types of tales that "experts" like to record and study. Yet all of this ferment in storytelling has gradually been manipulated by different groups until the dominant associations, influenced by the totalizing features of the culture industry, endeavor to control and decide what is good storytelling and how storytellers should be. The professionalization of storytelling has led to a situation that is very different from preliterate days, when the sharing of rituals, news, and wisdom was at the heart of storytelling, generally without a fee and without concern about copyrighting one's material.

Given the fact that storytelling can be profitable, many storytellers in Western societies make use of fairy tales because they know that children respond well to this genre. Moreover, they do not have to worry about obtaining permission for performing classical folk and fairy tales. Professional storytellers must worry about such matters, and they must know how to market themselves and their tales. Hence their attitudes toward their material and toward their audiences undergo a shift to the economic, to the commercial, and a story becomes a vehicle for achieving notoriety. For them, the fairy tale is not only about happiness; it is their means to obtain a modicum of happiness themselves.

But what about the children in their audiences? What about the adults? Are we to believe that their fairy tales will make a greater difference for us than the fairy-tale films in movie theaters, on television, and on our computer screens? Where do we go from here with all of these fairy-tale films and professional storytellers reacting with a vengeance against technology that might be misplaced?

Why all this fuss about fairy tales? Can fairy tales influence and change our lives?

I am tempted to say, "Read this book and you will find out," but I hear myself echoing those dazzling television commercials that encourage us to use a certain type of shampoo so that we can turn into handsome princes or beautiful princesses and live happily ever after.

1

Of Cats and Men

Framing the Civilizing Discourse
of the Fairy Tale

It is said that a man's best friend is his dog, but those of us who read fairy tales know better. Time and again, cats have come to the aid of poor, suffering young men, much more often than dogs. In two of the more famous examples, Charles Perrault's "Puss in Boots" (1697) and Mme. D'Aulnoy's "The White Cat" (1697), cats enabled disadvantaged and often maltreated youngest sons to attain wealth and power. In the case of "Puss in Boots," a miller's son becomes a rich marquis and marries the king's daughter, thanks to a cat. In "The White Cat," a young nobleman is helped by a strange, gracious cat, in reality a princess, who marries him and makes him a wealthy man. Indeed, there are hundreds if not thousands of oral folk tales and literary fairy tales throughout the world in which a cat either takes pity on an unfortunate young man or helps him advance in society.[1] Why, then, do we still proclaim that man's best friend is his dog? Is it because cats have frequently been associated with females and goddesses, and men must worship them or pay the consequences? Is it because men and women are supposedly opposites and often fight like cats and dogs? Is it because cats are allegedly duplicitous and devious and cannot be trusted? Or is it because cats have learned that men are dumb and ungrateful and not worth maintaining as friends?

Puss in Boots, illustrated by Gustav Doré, from *Les Contes de Perrault* (Paris: Hetzel, 1867)

It is difficult to answer these questions because the folklore about the relations between cats and men is so rich and varied. One need only glance at *Nine Lives: The Folklore of Cats* (1980), by the renowned British folklorist Katharine Briggs, or *The Folktale Cat* (1992), edited by the noted American scholar Frank de Caro, to ascertain this fact, to name but two of the more fascinating books on the subject.[2] Yet no matter how mysterious and variegated the folklore is, one aspect is clear: In both the oral and the literary tradition in Europe and America, cats play a very special role in *civilizing men* and in explaining how the civilizing process operates in Western society. In fact, I want to suggest that by studying the *literary* tradition of "Puss in Boots" from Giovan Francesco Straparola's 1550 version through Walt Disney's silent animated film of 1923, we can learn, thanks to an assortment of gifted cats, an immense amount about the sociohistorical origins of the literary fairy tale in the West and why honorable cats perhaps have decided not to be man's best friend.

To speak about the honor of cats in literary fairy tales necessitates redeeming the honor of two neglected writers of fairy tales, namely, Giovan Francesco Straparola and Giambattista Basile, and to set the record straight about the historical origins of fairy tales in the West. It also means grasping how the narrative discourse of the fairy tale as a genre was essentially framed by men who unconsciously and consciously set a gender-specific agenda for the manner in which we expect the miraculous turn of events to occur. If we study the formative "Puss in Boots" versions of Giovan Francesco Straparola, Giambattista Basile, and Charles Perrault, we shall see that the narrative strategies of these authors, the transformations of motifs and characters, the different styles, and the implied historical symbolical meanings and overtones constitute a generic mode of discourse that establishes the frame for the manner in which we discuss, debate, and propose standards of behavior and norms in Western civilization. As Marina Warner has demonstrated in her remarkable and comprehensive study, *From the Beast to the Blonde: On Fairytales and Their Tellers*,[3] it is a male frame that needs to be expanded and questioned if not subverted.

But let us begin by trying to understand how this frame may have originated, which means beginning with Giovan Francesco Straparola. Frankly, we do not know much about this man, but our lack of knowledge does not mean he deserves the neglect that he has suffered. In fact, he could even be called the "father" of the modern literary fairy tale in the West, for Straparola was the first truly gifted author to write numerous fairy tales in the vernacular and to cultivate a form and function for this kind of narrative that made it an acceptable genre among the educated classes in Italy and soon after in France, Germany, and England.

Straparola was born about 1480 in Caravaggio, a town in the region of Lombardy. His name may even be a pseudonym, for it means someone who is loquacious. Perhaps his family or friends used it as a nickname, or perhaps Straparola used the name in a satirical sense. Whatever the case may be, we do know that he moved to Venice and published a collection of sonnets under the title *Opera nova da Zoan Francesco Streparola da Caravazo novamente stampata Sonetti* in 1508. Forty-two years later, in 1550, the first part of his major work *Le Piacevoli Notti* (*Pleasant Nights*) appeared, followed by the second part in 1553. The work seemed to have met with a favorable reception because a second edition was printed in 1556, and by 1560 it had also been translated into French. Comments in the Italian editions indicate that Straparola probably died in 1558.

Straparola was not an original writer, but he was the first to make a substantial contribution to the shaping of the literary fairy tale and to give it a prominent place in his unusual collection of tales. The frame for the *Le Piacevoli Notti*, first translated into English as *The Facetious Nights* by W. G. Waters in 1894,[4] was modeled after Boccaccio's *Decameron* and had strong political implications. The prologue reveals how Ottoviano Maria Sforza, the bishop-elect of Lodi (most likely the real Sforza, who died in 1540) is compelled to leave Milan because of political plots against him. He takes his widowed daughter, Signora Lucretia, with him; and since her husband has died in 1523, we can assume that the setting for the *Nights* is sometime between 1523 and 1540. The bishop and his daughter flee first to Lodi, then to Venice, and finally settle on the island of Murano. They gather a small group of congenial people around them: ten gracious ladies, two matronly women, and four educated and distinguished gentlemen. Since it is Carnival time, Lucretia proposes that members of the company take turns telling stories during the two weeks before Lent, and consequently there are thirteen nights on which stories are told, amounting to seventy-four tales in all.

As was generally the case in upper-class circles, a formal social ritual is followed. Each night there is a dance by the young ladies. Then Lucretia draws five ladies' names from a vase, and those five are to tell the tales that evening. But before the storytelling, one of the men must sing a song, after which a lady tells a tale, followed by a riddle in verse. Most of the riddles are examples of the double entendre and have strong sexual connotations, especially those told by the men. The object is to discuss erotic subjects in a highly refined manner. During the course of the thirteen nights, a man is invited every now and then to replace a woman and tell a tale. In addition, Lucretia herself tells two tales.

There are very few "tragic" tales among the seventy-four, and the optimism, humor, and graceful style of the narratives may be due to the fact that Straparola was writing in Venice at a time when there was relative harmony in that society. To a certain extent, the fictional company on the island of Murano can be regarded as an ideal representation of how people can relate to one another and comment in pleasing and instructive ways about all types of experience. The stories created by Straparola are literary fairy tales, revised oral tales, anecdotes, erotic tales, buffo tales of popular Italian life, didactic tales, fables, and tales based on the work of writers who preceded him, such as Boccaccio, Franco Sacchetti, Ser Giovanni Forentino, Giovanni Sercambi, and others.

During the eleventh night, the lady Fordiana begins the storytelling by relating the first known literary version of "Puss in Boots" in Europe. Yet, as we shall see, there are no boots, and the cat is really not a cat. The story goes as follows:

There was once a poor woman in Bohemia named Soriana, who had three sons named Dusolino, Tesifone, and Constantino. Right before she dies, she leaves her two oldest sons a kneading trough and a pastry board and her youngest, Constantino, a cat. The older sons are able to earn a good living with their inheritance, but they treat Constantino cruelly and do not share anything with him. The cat, who is a fairy in disguise, takes pity on him and helps him by providing the king with rabbits and winning his good graces with many other gifts. Because the cat frequently returns to

Constantino with wonderful food and drink, the two older brothers are jealous, but there is nothing they can do. The cat cleans Constantino's blotched face with her tongue and eventually takes him to meet the king. When they near the castle, the cat tells Constantino to take off his clothes and jump into the river. Then the cat yells for help, and the king sends his men to rescue Constantino and dress him in noble garments. Of course, the king wants to know why the now good-looking young man almost drowned, and Constantino, who is baffled, must depend on the cat, who tells the king that Constantino was bringing a great treasure of jewels to the king when he was robbed and thrown into the river to drown. Impressed by Constantino's alleged wealth, the king arranges for him to marry his daughter. After the ceremonies and festivities, Constantino is given ten mules with gold and rich garments, and he is expected to take the princess and a group of other people to his castle, which he does not have. Again, the cat comes to his rescue by riding in advance and warning cavaliers, shepherds, and herdsmen to beware of a great troop of armed men. Unless they say they serve Master Constantino, they will be in trouble. Then the cat arrives at a castle, which is weakly defended. In fact, Signor Valentino, the lord of the castle, has recently died during a journey to seek his wife. So the cat easily convinces the guards and company of people at this castle to say they serve Constantino too. When Constantino finally arrives with his bride, he easily establishes himself as the lord of the castle. Soon after, the king of Bohemia dies, and Constantino inherits the throne. He and his wife have many children and live a long life. When they die, their children inherit the kingdom.

Although this tale alone cannot represent how the literary fairy tale came to be established and institutionalized in Europe, and although it cannot be considered representative of all the tales in Straparola's *Pleasant Nights*, I should nevertheless like to use it to illustrate a possible means for opening perspectives and questions about the origins of the literary fairy tale and the ramifications of such origination and institutionalization.

It is possible to approach this tale as a literary adaptation of an oral tale that may have been common in Italy, generally involving an animal that comes to the rescue of a forlorn human being, usually a man, who manages to pull himself up by his bootstraps in the end. Folklorists generally categorize this type as AT 545b "Puss in Boots." But the fact is, we do not know exactly what oral tale Straparola used as the basis for his literary narrative. We can only assume that he had heard some version of "Constantino" and decided to write his own. In other words, Straparola appropriated popular lore to represent it in his own manner and comment on the mores and values of his time. If we regard his tale as a mode of representation that was intended to indicate how a young man was to behave in a certain social situation, we see that it has a great deal to say about Venetian society of Straparola's time.

What are the important features of the tale?

1. A young peasant, who is ugly and has no manners, is placed at a disadvantage in life because he is poor and his mother leaves him nothing but a cat when she dies.
2. The cat, however, turns out to be a fairy, or his good fortune.
3. The cat endows him with good looks, clothes, and manners and puts him on display.
4. Only through her intercession, her good fortune and knowledge of the civilizing process, does Constantino have a chance of moving up in society, from a poor peasant to king of Bohemia.
5. The cat uses threats and the show of force to help Constantino succeed.
6. Constantino's climb is based on duplicity, spectacle (display of gifts, clothes, richness), a marriage of convenience, and patriarchal absolute rule. The king's word is the final word, and Constantino's word will also become absolute after he becomes king of Bohemia.

Using these features, we can draw some interesting parallels between the world of the tale and Venetian and Italian sixteenth-century society that have ramifications for the later development of the literary tradition. In many city and state republics in Italy, it was difficult but possible to rise from the lower classes and become a rich lord. Such advancement depended on making the right con-nections, luck, a good marriage, shrewdness, and the ability to wield power effectively. This kind of social mobility was more accessible to men than to women, and the social institutions cre-ated in the cities benefited men just as the family structure was cen-tered around the male as the seat of all power. Women's role was to grace the home and serve men, providing them with the means to establish themselves and their families.

Though "Constantino" features a poor, dismal peasant boy in Bohemia, there is little doubt that literate Italians of that time, who were very few and were from the upper classes, read the tale metaphorically as the "lucky" rise of a man who learns how to use the civilizing process to his advantage. In Straparola's version of the "Puss in Boots"–type tale, the highest virtue that a man can achieve is the status of lord or king, no matter what it takes. There is no real rational or moral basis for Constantino's rise and success, and the only thing that he must learn is how to fool other people, wear the right clothes, pretend to be what he is not, and take power through force. Clearly, the strategy of the narrative, the pur-poseful unfolding of the author's desire, is to rationalize and legiti-mate patriarchy; women play a key role, but they are dispensable in the end, just as they become dispensable at the end of *Pleasant Nights*, when Lent arrives and it is time to repent for one's sins.

Now, if Straparola set the scene for a particular literary manner in which the tales of cats and men were to be told, how did other authors consciously respond to this initial tale? Do we have proof that other writers knew of Straparola's tale and changed it to com-ment on their own times? Were they interested in representing power relations within the civilizing process?

The next literary version of the "Puss in Boots"–type tale was written by Giambattista Basile. We know a great deal about him, unlike Straparola, including the fact that he had probably read Straparola's "Constantino" and may have been familiar with other oral versions. But let us first turn to a quick synopsis of his version, "Cagliuso."

This tale concerns an old beggar in Naples who bequeaths his eldest son, Oraziello, a sieve so he can earn a living and his younger son, Cagliuso, a cat because he is the baby of the family. While Oraziello goes out into the world and begins to have success, Cagliuso bemoans his fate and worries that he now has two mouths to feed. However, the cat tells him, "You are complaining too soon, and you've more luck than wits! You don't know your good fortune, for I am able to make you rich if I put myself to it."

Cagliuso apologizes to her catship, who goes fishing and hunting and carries her catch to the king as humble presents from Lord Cagliuso. At one point the cat tells the king that Lord Cagliuso would like to place himself at the king's service and would like to visit him the next day. When the next day arrives, however, the cat tells the king that Cagliuso's servants have robbed him and left him without even a shirt to his back. In response, the king sends clothes to Cagliuso from his own wardrobe, and soon the beggar's son appears at the king's court dressed as a lord. A banquet is prepared, but the dumb Cagliuso can think only of regaining his proper beggarly rags, and the cat must constantly tell him to keep his mouth shut. Eventually, the cat manages to have a private conversation with the king in which she praises Cagliuso's intelligence and wealth and wants to arrange a marriage of convenience with the king's daughter. Since she knows that the king will want some proof of Cagliuso's immense wealth, the cat suggests that the king send trusty servants with her to Cagliuso's estates around Rome and Lombardy to procure information about the young man's situation. The cat runs ahead of the king's servants and threatens shepherds, gamekeepers, and farmers that robbers are on their way; if they do not say that everything belongs to Lord Cagliuso, they will be killed. Consequently, the king's servants hear the same message wherever they go and are convinced that Cagliuso owns a tremendous amount of property.

Now the king becomes anxious to bring about a marriage between his daughter and Cagliuso and promises the cat a rich reward if she can arrange everything, which she does. After an entire month of feasting, the cat advises Cagliuso to take his wife's dowry and buy some land in Lombardy. The beggar's son follows this advice and soon becomes a wealthy baron. He continually thanks the cat and promises her that whenever she should die, he will have her embalmed and placed inside a golden cage. To test Cagliuso, the cat pretends to die and learns how ungrateful her master is when Cagliuso wants to take her by the paws and simply throw her out the window. All at once the cat jumps up and exclaims, "Get out of my sight, and may a curse be on everything I've done for you because you're not even worth spitting on! What a fine golden cage you prepared for me! What a beautiful grave you've assigned me! I go and serve you, work and sweat, only to receive this reward. Oh, woe is he who boils his pot for the hope of others! That philosopher put it well when he said, 'Whoever goes to bed an ass wakes up an ass.'"[5]

Though Cagliuso tries to make amends, the cat runs through the door and keeps on running while muttering the following moral to end the tale:

> Oh God keep you from those rich men turned poor
> And from beggars grown rich who now have more.[6]

As we can see, Basile's version of "Puss in Boots" is immensely different from Straparola's, and obviously the changes have a lot to do with the different life that Basile led and wanted to represent. Born in Naples in 1576, Basile came from a middle-class family and spent his youth in his native city. In 1600 he took a trip to Venice, where he became a soldier to earn a living and began writing poetry. By 1609 he had begun publishing his poetry, and thanks to his sister, a famous singer, he was appointed to a position at the court of Mantua in 1613. After that, throughout his life, Basile held various positions as administrator or magistrate. In 1620 he returned to Naples and was appointed a captain in Lagonegro. He continued to be successful as a poet and became a member of various literary academies. Yet it was not his poetry that would make him famous but his book of fairy tales in Neapolitan prose dialect. He began writing this book, titled *Lo Cunto de li Cunti* (*The Tale of Tales*) in the early 1630s, but unfortunately he never saw the published version, for he died of a disease contracted during an epidemic in 1632. His sister arranged for the publication of *Lo Cunto de li Cunti*, which appeared in four separate books between 1634 and 1636. When the fourth edition was published in 1674, the title of the collection of tales was changed to *Il Pentamerone*.

Like Straparola, Basile set a frame for his tales, but unlike Straparola, he used a fairy tale as his "tale of tales" to set the stage for fifty marvelous stories. In this frame tale, Zoza, the daughter of the king of Vallepelosa, cannot laugh, and her father is so concerned about her happiness that he invites people from all over the world to try to make her laugh. Yet nobody can succeed until an old woman who attempts to sop up oil in front of the palace has her jug broken by a mischievous court page. The ensuing argument between the old woman and the page, each hurling coarse and vulgar epithets at one another, is so delightful that Zoza bursts into laughter. However, this laughter angers the old woman, and she curses Zoza, saying, "Be off with you, and may you never see the bud of a husband unless it is the Prince of Camporotondo!"[7] To her dismay, Zoza learns that this prince, named Tadeo, is under the spell of a wicked fairy and is in a tomb. He can only be wakened and liberated by a woman who fills with her tears a pitcher that is hanging on a nearby wall.

In need of help, Zoza visits three different fairies and receives a walnut, a chestnut, and a hazelnut as gifts. Then she goes to Tadeo's tomb and weeps into the pitcher for two days. When the pitcher is almost full, she falls asleep because she is tired from all the crying. While she is sleeping, however, a slave girl steals the pitcher, fills it, wakens Tadeo, and takes the credit for bringing him back to life. Tadeo marries her, and she becomes pregnant.

But Zoza, whose happiness depends on Tadeo, is not about to concede the prince to a slave girl. She rents a house across from Tadeo's palace and manages to attract Tadeo's attention. However, the slave girl threatens to beat the baby if Tadeo spends any time with Zoza, who now uses another tactic to gain entrance into Tadeo's palace. On three different occasions she opens the nuts. One contains a little dwarf who sings; the next twelve chickens made of gold; and the third a doll that spins gold. The slave girl demands these fascinating objects, and Tadeo sends for them, offering Zoza whatever she wants. To his surprise, Zoza gives the objects as gifts. Yet the final one, the doll, stirs an uncontrollable passion in the slave girl to hear stories during her pregnancy, and she threatens Tadeo again: unless women come to tell her tales, she will kill their unborn baby. So Tadeo invites ten women from the rabble known for their storytelling: lame Zeza, twisted Cecca, goitered Meneca, big-nosed Tolla, hunchback Popa, drooling Antonella, snout-faced Ciulla, rheumy Paola, mangy Ciommetella, and diarrhetic Iacoba. The women spend the day chattering and gossiping, and after the evening meal, one tale is told by each of the ten for five nights. Finally, on the last day, Zoza is invited to tell the last tale, and she recounts what happened to her. The slave girl tries to stop her, but Tadeo insists that Zoza be allowed to tell the tale to the end. When he realizes that Zoza's tale is true, Tadeo has the pregnant slave girl buried alive, and he marries Zoza to bring the tale of tales to a happy conclusion.

If we were to compare just the frame tales of Straparola's *Notti* and Basile's *Pentamerone*, it is again apparent that there are major differences between the two. Basile is much more witty, vulgar, and complex than Straparola. He wrote in a mannered Neapolitan dialect to address a new reading public that had begun to form at the beginning of the sixteenth century and was not interested in the courtly culture of representation. This reading public was open to dialect and materials from the oral culture. According to Barbara Broggini,[8] Basile shifted the perspective of the folk tale so that both the peasant and aristocratic classes are critiqued. For instance, the value system of civility is transformed in the tales to favor the standards of the rising middle classes that were in the process of establishing their interests throughout Italy. As a consequence, Basile parodied the peasantry and condemned the corruption of court society, arguing for self-determination and the ethics of fairness through hard work. One of the reasons why Basile chose dialect and popular tales is that he could incorporate many levels of meaning in these tales and escape aristocratic censorship.

If we now return to "Cagliuso," we can see that there is definitely a shift in ideological perspective and style from Straparola's

"Constantino." Whereas Straparola celebrated the good fortune of a deprived young man who is the hero of his story and represents the continuity of patriarchal rule as the new king of Bohemia, Basile focuses on the cat as the "tragicomic" heroine who serves a stupid and ungrateful peasant and a greedy and gullible king. Caught in the middle, the cat can literally be taken for a middle-class protagonist who speaks for a middle-class morality (not to mention, the role of women). In some ways, the cat's situation resembles that of Basile, who was expected to act as an administrator of the popular class while serving the whims of the aristocracy. The cat's power is not "magic," like that of the fairy cat in Straparola's tale, but resides in her shrewdness, cunning, and industry. She knows the court is interested in nothing but show (clothing) and wealth, and she also knows that it is important to have the right manners and speech if one is to succeed in society. She takes pride in her work, her ability to arrange contracts and to maintain loyalty, and she expects only justice and due compensation in return. When she realizes that Cagliuso will behave like any other rich lord, she parts company with him for good.

Basile's tale, though humorous, contains a devastating critique of the feudal system of his time and represents a moral code that was not yet fully instituted within the civilizing process in Europe. Throughout the tale the cat is completely loyal to her master, works hard, and demonstrates that wits are more important than fortune. Indeed, the cat saves her own life and sees through the facade of the servant-master relationship because she is smart and knows how to use the feudal system to her advantage. The difficulty is that she cannot achieve the security that she would like— and that Basile apparently also desired.

This lack of gratitude and security is not the case with Charles Perrault's cat, the famous Puss in Boots, the first literary cat to wear boots. Indeed, the security and destiny of this master cat may be due to the fact that the high bourgeoisie was more secure and respected at Louis XIV's court, as was Perrault himself. Though the aristocracy established most of the rules and behavioral codes in the civilizing process of the ancien régime, the norms and values of civilité, and their modalities, would have been impossible to maintain without the cooperation of the middle classes.

Perrault himself was an important administrator, a member of the Academie Française, a noteworthy poet, and a cultural critic who challenged Nicolas Boileau's theories in the controversial *Quarrels of the Ancients and the Moderns*. Perrault regarded himself as a modernist and wanted to break away from the neoclassicist rules dependent on Greco-Roman models; he published his famous *Histoires ou Contes du temps passé* (*Stories or Tales of Past Times*) in 1697 in part to prove that France had its own unique traditions that could be cultivated in innovative ways. In fact, the fairy tale had gradually become *en vogue* during the 1690s, and Perrault was only one among many writers in the literary salons to begin promoting this genre. The other prominent writers were mostly women. Mme. D'Aulnoy, Mlle. L'Héritier, Mlle. de La Force, Mme. Lubert, and Mlle. Bertrand all published important collections of tales to establish the genre as a literary institution, but we remember Perrault mainly because, I suggest, the frame for our reception of the tales was set by male writers, who have more or less marked the ways in which we are to interpret and analyze them. Certainly, male writers have inscribed their concerns and desires in such a way that they play a role in determining our readings of the tales.

Let us take Perrault's "The Master Cat or Puss in Boots." As Denise Escarpit has demonstrated in her immense study, *Histoire d'un Conte: Le Chat Botté en France et en Angleterre*, there is a strong probability that Perrault knew the literary versions of Straparola and Basile,[9] and he most likely knew some of the oral versions that had become common in France. Whatever the case may be, Perrault was not satisfied with those stories, and by writing his own version, he entered into a dialogue with them and sought to articulate his position regarding the position of the cat, his hero, as a mediator between a miller's son and a king. Again it is important to review the essential components of the plot.

A miller dies and bequeaths his three sons, respectively, a mill, an ass, and a cat. The youngest son is so dissatisfied with inheriting the cat that he wants to eat it and make a muff of its skin. To

Puss in Boots, illustrated by Gustav Doré, from *Les Contes de Perrault* (Paris: Hetzel, 1867)

save his life, the cat responds, "Don't trouble yourself, master. Just give me a pouch and a pair of boots to go into the bushes, and you'll see that you were not left with as bad a share as you think."[10]

The extraordinary cat goes into the woods, where he proceeds to catch rabbits, partridges, and other game, and he gives them to the king as presents from the Marquis de Carrabas. On a day when the cat knows the king will be taking a drive on the banks of a river with his daughter, the cat instructs his master to take off his clothes and bathe in the river. When the king comes by, the cat pretends that robbers have taken his master's clothes. Consequently, the king provides the miller's son with royal clothes, and the princess immediately falls in love with him. The young man gets into the royal coach, while the cat runs ahead and warns peasants, who are mowing and reaping in the fields, that if they do not say that the estate belongs to the Marquis de Carrabas, they will be cut into tiny pieces like minced meat. Of course the peasants obey, and in the meantime the cat arrives at a beautiful castle owned by an ogre. He flatters the ogre, who can change himself into anything he wants, by asking him to transform himself into a lion. Then he dares the ogre to change himself into a rat or mouse, and after the ogre performs this feat, he is promptly eaten by the cat. When the king, his daughter, and the miller's son arrive at this beautiful castle, they are all overwhelmed by its splendor, and after the king has had five or six cups of wine, he proposes that the marquis become his son-in-law. No fool, the "marquis" accepts, and after he marries the princess, the cat becomes a great lord and never again runs after mice except for his own amusement.

Perrault's version combines elements of the Straparola and Basile tales to forge his own statement, which he presents in two ironic verse morals at the end of his tale:

> *Although the advantage may be great*
> *When one inherits a grand estate*
> *From father handed down to son,*
> *Young men will find that industry*
> *Combined with ingenuity,*
> *Will lead to prosperity.*

Another Moral

> *If the miller's son had quick success*
>   *In winning such a fair princess,*
> *By turning on the charm,*
> *Then regard his manners, looks, and dress*
>   *That inspired her deepest tenderness,*
> *For they can't do one any harm.*[11]

These morals reflect two of the major themes in Perrault's tale that were also significant in the tales of Straparola and Basile. In the first instance, Perrault asserts that the best means of becoming a rich nobleman is brains and industry. In the second instance, he maintains that show and the proper clothing (spectacle and display) can also enable a man from the lower classes to move up in society. But Perrault deals with more than just these two themes in his tale: He also demonstrates that speech and writing can be used to attain power within the civilizing process.

In his highly perceptive essay, *"Puss-in-Boots:* Power of Signs—Signs of Power," Louis Marin points out that

> the cat is an operator of change: he articulates a spatial continuum that differentiates space by a temporal program or better strategy. The cat as trickster figure in North American Indian myths is always wandering in the different parts of the world. But his trips in our tale cannot be separated from his tricks. I mean his use of language. This use is manifested in the tale by the fact that the cat always anticipates his master's itinerary toward the cultural (social and economic) maximum. Everything occurs as if his master's coming in a place actualizes what his cat says just before. Textually speaking, the cat is the representative of the narrative modalizations (mainly the modality of desire) and his master, the vehicle of narrative assertions (or wish fulfillments).[12]

It is not only the manipulation of speech within the tale that outlines how men can succeed in society; it is in Perrault's very writing of the text itself that generic prescriptions take hold, assume power, and become established models for reading and writing. If we begin by examining the text, it becomes evident that Perrault's tale consolidates crucial elements from the Straparola and Basile versions to transform the cat into the *master cat*, whose story effaces all those before it and determines the direction of all those to come. Perrault's Puss demonstrates what it takes for a middle-class administrator to succeed in French society of his time:

1. Loyalty and obedience to one's master; otherwise one will be killed;
2. the proper tools to do one's job; the cat needs a pouch to capture his prey and boots of respectability to gain entrée to the king's castle;
3. gracious speech that is also duplicitous;
4. cunning to take advantage of those who are more powerful;
5. the acquisition of land and wealth by force;
6. the readiness to kill when necessary;
7. the ability to arrange business affairs such as a marriage of convenience that will lead to permanent security.

In the process, it is important to note that women are pushed to the margins in this tale, just as they are in the real world of men. They exist as display, as chattel, as bargaining items. They are speechless. The words of the cat that generate and mediate the action are crucial for attaining success. The cat knows how to plead, flatter, advise, threaten, dupe, and generate a proposition from the opposing side.

But we must remember that these are the words of Perrault, who manipulated, arranged, and played with them on the page. In one of the most thorough and insightful readings of Perrault's tales in recent years, Philip Lewis demonstrates that Perrault was strongly influenced by Descartes and developed a "rationalist aesthetics" that was the governing principle in all his tales.[13] Yet Perrault did not slavishly incorporate Cartesian ideas into his aesthetics. Lewis comments,

> By forgetting the vigilant rigor with which Descartes structures and verifies the passage from saying to seeing, by dispensing with the methodic analysis of experience in the service of truth in favor of constructing elaborate comparisons and analogies that promote an accommodation of reason with verisimilitude, Perrault manages to restructure the relation of the verbal to the visual, enabling them to function as the polar terms of a reciprocal exchange. That drastic relaxation of the foundationalist, scientific impulse is perhaps typical of what happens to philosophical reflection in the hands of a so-called man of letters; it is certainly anticipatory of the pattern that thinkers from the eighteenth century onward would appropriate in representing the passage of ideas into art as a process of sublimation.[14]

The dominant perspective in Perrault's tales is the result of a compromise formation "in which a simple, mainstream rationalism accredits a stable, technological continuist account of knowledge as well-formed representation."[15] On the one hand, this means that Perrault's compromise of Cartesian rationalism served to represent the magnificence of King Louis XIV and his court, that is, to reinforce the ideological import of courtly manners and mores and the dominance of French language and culture. On the other hand, Perrault did not force "the transcendental model that would finally assimilate all cognitive experience of the subject to conception modeled on the forming of an image,"[16] but he left room for reflection and resistance to this model, making his tales somewhat ambivalent. This ambivalence is crucial to the appeal of his tales because it creates subtle and profound contradictions. However, I argue that it is Perrault's compromising mentality, which seeks to legitimate the power of patriarchal order, that demands our attention, for this mentality generates a rational aesthetics that feeds into the domestication of the fairy tale in the nineteenth century and its commodification in the twentieth century. Of course, the aesthetics of literary fairy tales and their function within the civilizing process cannot be traced entirely to Perrault. Nevertheless, his case is highly indicative of a certain mode of thinking and writing basic to the approach that many Western authors after him took. Perrault carefully contemplated known literary and oral versions of fairy tales, changed them in his mind and on paper, represented his own society and literary debates to himself and his readers, and sought to endow his words with the power of conviction so that they might become exemplary.

And become exemplary they did. Almost all of the eight tales that he published in *Histoires ou Contes du temps passé*—"Sleeping Beauty," "Cinderella," "Little Red Riding Hood," "Little Tom Thumb," "Bluebeard," "Riquet with the Tuft," "The Fairies," and "Puss in Boots"—have become classics in Western society. And his verse tales, "The Foolish Wishes" and "Donkey-Skin," have also achieved classical status. In the case of "Puss in Boots," the tale was disseminated through chapbooks and broadsides at the very beginning of the eighteenth century, translated into English and German by 1730, and became firmly embedded in the oral tradition. Obviously, there were many different versions that continued to be told and spread, but for the most part, the literary tradition of "Puss in Boots" was now based mainly on Perrault's version. For all intents and purposes, the versions of Straparola and Basile were erased from Western memory. Indeed, they were no longer necessary, for Perrault's literary text became the standard-bearer of a male civilizing process at a time when French culture was setting the dominant cultural standards in Europe, and at a time when the fairy tale was being firmly established as a literary institution by Perrault and numerous other French writers.

It is interesting to note that by the time the Brothers Grimm began publishing their collection of fairy tales in 1812, they reproduced a version of "Puss in Boots" that was very similar to Perrault's.[17] In fact, they decided to drop the tale from their collection because it was either too much within the French literary tradition or too commonly known as a literary tale to be considered a "true" folk tale. Although nobody could claim true authorship or ownership of "Puss in Boots" by the nineteenth century because it had been appropriated in many different ways by both the literary and oral traditions, it is important to note that the dominant paradigm resembled Perrault's tale. In other words, that version became the classical reference point or touchstone in publishing and in oral folklore, and it did not matter whether the tale was attributed to or signed by Perrault because his signature and his social-class and gender signatures had become deeply woven into the tale itself through the relations between cat and master. Furthermore, the tale became one of many more or less fixed classical tales like "Sleeping Beauty," "Cinderella," and "Little Red Riding Hood" that have determined the manner in which we socialize children and ourselves and set up "civilized" standards of behavior in the West. It is a male frame that is not entirely rigid, but it is within this enunciated symbolical code and order, whether oral or literary, that we discuss and debate norms, values, and gender roles.

Whether for children or adults, fairy tales in all forms have played and continue to play a crucial role in the socialization process and in aesthetic development. The genre of the fairy tale has developed through oral, literary, and cinematic means, and "Puss in Boots" again enables us to grasp how the frame for our absorption and appropriation of fairy tales is determined through a male denominator in the films and videos of the twentieth century. Here the case of Walt Disney is very important. Of all the early animators, Disney was the one who truly revolutionized the fairy tale as institution through the cinema. One could almost say that he was obsessed by the fairy-tale genre, or to put it another way, Disney felt drawn to fairy tales because they reflected his own struggles in life. After all, Disney came from a relatively poor family; suffered from the exploitative and stern treatment of an unaffectionate father; was spurned by his early sweetheart; and became a success through his tenacity, cunning, and courage and his ability to gather talented artists and managers such as his brother Roy.

One of his early films, "Puss in Boots" (1922), produced in Kansas City, is crucial for understanding his approach to the literary fairy tale and how he used it as a form of self-figuration that would mark the genre for years to come. As Russell Merritt and J. B. Kaufman remark, "In many ways, Disney's first films in Kansas City seem as accomplished as his later Hollywood silents. We have to wait several years to find a film as well-paced, as thematically rich, or with backgrounds as provocative and well-drawn as his earliest surviving Laugh-O-Gram fairy tales such as 'Little Red Riding Hood,' 'Puss in Boots,' and 'Cinderella.'"[18] In the case of "Puss in Boots" Disney did not especially care whether one knew the original Perrault text or some other popular version. It is also unclear which text he actually knew. However, what is clear is that Disney sought to replace all earlier versions with his animated version and that his cartoon is astonishingly autobiographical.

The hero is a young man, a commoner, who is in love with the king's daughter, and she fondly returns his affection. At the same time, the hero's black cat, a female, is having a romance with the royal white cat, who is the king's chauffeur. When the gigantic king discovers that the young man is wooing his daughter, he kicks him out of the palace, followed by Puss. At first, the hero does not want puss's help, nor will he buy her the boots that she sees in a shop window. Then they go to the movies together and see a film with Rudolph Vaselino, a reference to the famous Rudolph Valentino, as a bullfighter that spurs Puss's imagination. She tells the hero that she now has an idea that will help him win the king's daughter, providing he will buy her the boots. Of course, the hero will do anything to obtain the king's daughter, and after he disguises himself as a masked bullfighter, Puss explains to him that she will use a hypnotic machine behind the scenes so he can defeat the bull and win the approval of the king. When the day of the bullfight arrives, the masked hero struggles but eventually manages to defeat the bull. The king is so overwhelmed by his performance that he offers his daughter's hand in marriage, but first he wants to know who the masked champion is. When the hero reveals himself, the king is enraged, but the hero grabs the princess and leads her to the king's chauffeur. The white cat jumps in the front seat of the car with Puss, and they speed off with the king vainly chasing after them.

Although Puss as cunning cat is crucial in this film, Disney focuses most of his attention on the young man who wants to succeed at all costs. In contrast to the traditional fairy tale, the hero is not a peasant, nor is he dumb. Read as a "parable" of Disney's life at that moment, the hero can be seen as young Disney wanting to break into the industry of animated films (the king) with the help of Ub Iwerks (Puss), his friend and best collaborator at that time. The hero upsets the king and runs off with his prize possession, the virginal princess. Thus, the king is dispossessed, and the young man outraces him with the help of his friends.

But Disney's film is also an attack on the literary tradition of the fairy tale. He robs the literary tale of its voice and changes its form and meaning. Since the cinematic medium is a popular form of expression and accessible to the public at large, Disney actually returns the fairy tale to the majority of people. The images (scenes, frames, characters, gestures, jokes) are readily comprehensible to young and old alike and to different social classes. In fact, the fairy tale is practically infantilized, just as the jokes are infantile. The plot records the deepest oedipal desire of every young boy: The son humiliates and undermines the father and runs off with his most valued object of love, the daughter/wife. By semiotically simplifying the Oedipus complex in black-and-white drawings and making fun of it so that it had a common appeal, Disney also touched on other themes:

1. Democracy—the film is very *American* in its attitude toward royalty. The monarchy is debunked, and a commoner causes a kind of revolution.

2. Technology—it is through the new technological medium of the movies that Puss's mind is stimulated. Then she uses a hypnotic machine to defeat the bull and another fairly recent invention, the automobile, to escape the king.

3. Modernity—the setting is obviously the twentieth century, and the modern minds are replacing the ancient. The revolution takes place as the king is outpaced, and he will be replaced by a commoner who knows how to use the latest inventions.

But who is this commoner? Was Disney making a statement on behalf of the masses? Was Disney celebrating "everyone" or "every man"? Did Disney believe in revolution and social change in the name of socialism? The answer to all these questions is simply "no."

Disney's hero is the enterprising young man, the entrepreneur, who uses technology to his own advantage. He does nothing to help the people or the community. In fact, he deceives the masses and the king by creating the illusion that he is stronger than the bull. He has learned, with the help of Puss, that one can achieve glory through deception. It is through the artful use of images that one can sway audiences and gain their favor. Animation is trickery—trick films—for still images are made to seem as if they move through automatization. As long as one controls the images (and machines) one can reign supreme, just as the hero is safe as long as he is disguised. The pictures conceal the controls and machinery. They prevent the audience from really viewing the production and manipulation, and in the end, audiences can no longer envision a fairy tale for themselves, as they can when they read one. The pictures deprive the audience of the ability to visualize their own characters, roles, and desires. At the same time, Disney offsets the deprivation with the pleasure of scopophilia and inundates the viewer with delightful images, humorous figures, and erotic signs. In general, the animator, Disney, projects the enjoyable fairy tale of his life through his own images, and he realizes through animated stills the basic oedipal dream that he was to play out time and again in most of his fairy-tale films. The repetition of Disney's infantile quest—the core of American mythology—enabled him to strike a chord in American viewers from the 1920s to the present, a chord that has also resounded across the ocean in Europe, for Disney continued framing the discourse of civility within a male frame in the tradition of writers like Straparola, Basile, Perrault, the Brothers Grimm, Ludwig Bechstein, Henri Pourrat, J. R. R. Tolkien, and C. S. Lewis as well as illustrators like George Cruikshank, Gustav Doré, Richard Doyle, Walter Crane, Charles Folkard, Arthur Rackham, and Charles Robinson. All of these men bonded, so to speak, or collaborated for the same reason: to use cats for their own self-figuration and to rationalize the manner in which power relations are distributed to benefit men in Western society.

Perhaps this is why cats are not man's best friend. In the literary and cinematic fairy-tale tradition of "Puss in Boots," they have been manipulated to extol male prowess and to represent the difficulties of middle-class writers and administrators in establishing a secure position for themselves in societies that are dominated by display and force. The only writer who spoke for cats and against servility was Basile, but who remembers his version? Who remembers his smart cat who long ago grasped the duplicity of the men who tried to frame her life? She escaped the frame, but the tradition of "Puss in Boots" reveals how the origins of this frame and its borders of enclosure are still very much with us as we approach the twenty-first century.

2

The Rationalization
of Abandonment
and Abuse in Fairy Tales

The Case of Hansel and Gretel

There are very few children, parents, or critics in Europe and America who do not know the fairy tale "Hansel and Gretel," by those famous brothers Jacob and Wilhelm Grimm. In fact, "Hansel and Gretel" has always been a worldwide favorite, and in a recent poll in Germany it was voted the number one fairy tale in the country. An entire book has been devoted to the story, *Deutung und Bedeutung von "Hänsel und Gretel"* by Regina Böhm-Korff,[1] which examines the myriad ways in which the tale has been interpreted, revised, and parodied. Apparently "Hansel and Gretel" is so rich in meaning that critics of all schools have been tempted time and again to explore every possible symbol and word in order to explain why we are fascinated by this narrative and why it has become fixed in the literary canon of Western countries as one of the great fairy-tale classics of all time. It is as though we can assume that "Hansel and Gretel" has always been with us, deeply embedded in our Western cultural tradition and collective unconscious. Presumably it will stay with us forever because it touches on essential universal desires and needs.

Yet such assumptions about "Hansel and Gretel" are fallacious, and most interpretations of the tale, though often stimulating,

Hansel and Gretel, illustrated by Hermann Vogel, from *Kinder- und Hausmärchen gesammelt durch die Brüder Grimm* (Munich: Braun and Schneider, 1894)

conceal the manner in which children as readers and listeners are abused through the scripting of the text, its transformations by the Grimms, and interpretations by scholars that rationalize child abuse in the name of the symbolic order of the father. We pretend to know all about "Hansel and Gretel" because we live by assumptions that have a scholarly veneer but actually promote ignorance. We appropriate assumptions because we have been taught that a certain popular tradition is not to be questioned but to be absorbed and appreciated. We lose sight, however, of the fact that the foundations of this tradition were created through particular human efforts and struggles at a particular time and place by humans seeking to inscribe themselves in history.

In the case of "Hansel and Gretel," the history of the text reveals how assiduously the Grimms, particularly Wilhelm, sought through the creation and re-creation of a fairy tale to make their mark on history and to influence our notions of socialization and the rearing of children. Moreover, the history of how readers have received their text demonstrates that we have avoided dealing with the disturbing problems that this fairy tale conveys and at the same time rationalizes. There has always been a close connection between the rationalization process of writing and the reception of fairy tales. How we interpret and use fairy tales in our daily lives, that is, our attitudes toward children and our treatment of children, has been scripted and prescribed to a great degree in the fairy tales themselves. To trace the social history of the scripting of "Hansel and Gretel" is thus to dislodge false assumptions about what we hold to be true and good about this tale and to probe the reasons why our celebration of the happy end of the tale is more ambivalent than we may want to believe.

The History of the Grimms' Text

When we begin talking about the Grimms' text of "Hansel and Gretel," we must first ask certain questions. Are we talking about the Ölenberg manuscript[2] of 1810, in which Wilhelm recorded an oral tale told by Dortchen Wild, who was later to become his wife? Are we talking about the 1812 printed version, in which the mother of the children is still their actual mother as was the case in the manuscript of 1810? Are we talking about the second edition of 1819, in which Wilhelm made numerous changes, including the transformation of the mother into a stepmother? Are we talking about the fifth edition of 1843, in which Wilhelm again made major changes based on his reading of the renowned Alsatian scholar August Stöber's tale "Das Eierkuchenhäuslein"[3] ("The Little Pancake House," 1842), written in dialect? Or are we talking about the final version of 1857, the consummate narrative that contained all of Wilhelm's stylistic and thematic changes?

Actually, to discuss and interpret any one of Wilhelm Grimm's texts necessitates knowing all of them and realizing that we are dealing not with a "pure" oral tradition that may have mythic roots in German or European culture but with a literary fairy-tale tradition connected to folklore that was part of a civilizing process involving discourses about norms, values, mores, and etiquette as well as depictions of actual social conditions. Given the fact that most of our references to "Hansel and Gretel" are generally to the 1857 text or some variation of it, we must ask how the Grimms arrived at that version, and how their creative process is significant for us today.

It is now common knowledge among literary historians and critics that the stories in the Grimms' *Kinder- und Hausmärchen* (*Children's and Household Tales*) cannot be considered "genuine" oral folk tales by any stretch of the imagination. The brothers, erudite scholars, were strongly influenced by literary tales and reshaped all of the stories they recorded from informants, who were not always from the peasantry. In the case of "Hansel and Gretel," Wilhelm heard the story from Dortchen Wild, daughter of a pharmacist of Huguenot descent and familiar with French fairy tales, and when he wrote it down as part of the Ölenberg manuscript, he entitled the tale "Das Brüderchen und das Schwesterchen" ("The Little Brother and the Little Sister"). This tale is very short, and the paratactic sentence structure is for the most part without fluent transitions and devoid of direct speech. There are numerous ellipses and very little description. For instance, the tale begins as follows: "There was once a poor woodcutter, who lived on the edge of a large forest. His life was so miserable that he could hardly nourish his wife and two children. One time he ran out of bread and was very afraid. That evening his wife spoke to him in bed: Take the two children early tomorrow morning and lead them into the large forest. Give them whatever bread is left, and make them a large fire. After that go away and leave them alone. The husband did not want to do this, but the wife did not leave him in peace until he finally agreed."[4]

The father and mother take the children into the woods two times. The children, who are not named, are abandoned the second time, wander in the forest, and find a house made of bread. The roof is covered with cakes, and the windows are made of sugar. The small old woman who seemingly befriends them is not referred to as a witch, but she is deceitful. She places Hansel in a stall to be fattened like a pig, but he pretends to remain thin by showing her a bone instead of his finger. After four weeks, the old woman becomes impatient and wants to bake him. Instead, the sister pushes her into the oven. At this point she is called a witch and burned to death. The story ends simply as follows: "They found the whole little house full of jewels. They filled their pockets with them and brought them to their father who became a rich man. However, their mother had died."[5]

This manuscript version was edited a great deal for the first printed edition of 1812. Jacob changed the title to "Hansel and Gretel," and Wilhelm did extensive editing so that the style of the tale flowed more smoothly, and well-known proverbs were added. Moreover, he made various substantial changes in the plot. For instance, the children call upon God for help twice; the old woman is portrayed as a witch from the very beginning; Hansel is fed like a chicken. The Grimms indicated in their notes that they knew Charles Perrault's "Le Petit Poucet" (1697), which has a similar plot, as well as other folk versions. By the time Wilhelm wrote the next version for the second edition of 1819, he was also familiar with Giambattista Basile's "Ninnillo and Nennella" (1634), in which a wicked stepmother is cruelly punished for causing the separation of a brother and sister. Indeed, in the 1819 edition the mother was transformed into a stepmother, along with many other changes that embellished the tale. However, the most dramatic changes occurred in the fifth edition of 1843, after Wilhelm had read Stöber's Alsatian tale "The Little Pancake House." What is fascinating here is that Stöber collected his tale from an informant who probably had read or heard the Grimms' literary version of "Hansel and Gretel" and had changed it for his or her purposes. Stöber himself cites the Grimms' edition as his literary source. (Interestingly, one of Stöber's changes is the transformation of the stepmother back into the biological mother, who does not die but greets the children with her husband at the end. Both parents regret what they did to the children.) Wilhelm, who had read Stöber's collection of tales, *Elsässisches Volksbüchlein* (1842), reappropriated certain phrases, sayings, and verses from the Alsatian dialect that he believed would lend his tale a more quaint and folksy tone. By the time the last edition of *Kinder- und Hausmärchen* was printed in 1857, Wilhelm had made so many changes in style and theme that the tale was twice as long as the original manuscript. For instance, in this final version, the tale begins this way:

A poor woodcutter lived with his wife and his two children on the edge of a large forest. The boy was called Hansel and the girl Gretel. The woodcutter did not have much food around the house, and when a great famine devastated the entire country, he could no longer provide enough for his family's daily meals. One night, as he was lying in bed and thinking about his worries, he began tossing and turning. Then he sighed and said to his wife, "What's to become of us? How can we feed our poor children when we don't even have enough for ourselves?"

"I'll tell you what," answered his wife. "Early tomorrow morning we'll take the children out into the forest where it's most dense. We'll build a fire and give them each a piece of bread. Then we'll go about our work and leave them alone. They won't find their way back home, and we'll be rid of them."

"No, wife," the man said. "I won't do this. I don't have the heart to leave my children in the forest. The wild beasts would soon come and tear them apart."

"Oh, you fool!" she said. "Then all four of us will have to starve to death. You'd better start planing the boards for our coffins!" She continued to harp on this until he finally agreed to do what she suggested.[6]

And instead of ending abruptly when the witch is killed, as in the manuscript of 1810, the tale ends as follows:

Since they no longer had anything to fear, they went into the witch's house, and there they found chests filled with pearls and jewels all over the place.

"They're certainly much better than pebbles," said Hansel, and he put whatever he could fit into his pockets, and Gretel said, "I'm going to carry some home too," and she filled her apron full of jewels and pearls.

"We'd better be on our way now," said Hansel, "so we can get out of the witch's forest."

When they had walked for a few hours, they reached a large river.

"We can't get across," said Hansel. "I don't see a bridge or any way over it."

"There are no boats either," Gretel responded, "but there's a white duck swimming over there. It's bound to help us across if I ask it." Then she cried out:

> *"Help us, help us, little duck!*
> *It's Hansel and Gretel, and we're really stuck.*
> *We can't get over, try as we may.*
> *Please take us across right away!"*

The little duck came swimming up to them, and Hansel got on top of its back and told his sister to sit down beside him.

"No," Gretel answered. "That will be too heavy for the little duck. Let it carry us across one at a time."

The kind little duck did just that, and when they were safely across and had walked for some time, the forest became more and more familiar to them, and finally they caught sight of their father's house from afar. They began to run at once, and soon rushed into the house and threw themselves around their father's neck. The man had not had a single happy hour since he had abandoned his children in the forest, and in the meantime his wife had died. Gretel opened and shook out her apron so that the pearls and jewels bounced about the room, and Hansel added to this by throwing one handful after another from his pocket. Now all their troubles were over, and they lived together in utmost joy.

My tale is done. See the mouse run. Catch it, whoever can, and then you can make a big cap out of its fur.[7]

In her comprehensive study of the different versions of "Hansel and Gretel," Böhm-Korff maintains that despite the various changes made by Wilhelm, there are certain "Urbilder," or "primordial images," such as the brother and sister as a pair, the witch, the witch's house, and the woods that have been constantly used by different interpreters as referential signs and that provide a certain stability in the search of a meaning. For Böhm-Korff, the core meaning of the tale can be found in the abandonment of children, and this meaning is connected to the treatment of children during the times in which the Grimms lived. Yet in my estimation, though this abandonment is very important for understanding the narrative, it is secondary to the *rationalization* of abandonment and abuse in Wilhelm's final text and in the manner that we have received "Hansel and Gretel" up to the present.

But before I discuss this point, I want to review what I consider to be the fundamental changes made by Wilhelm and to suggest why he may have made these changes. My comparisons will be based on the Ölenberg manuscript of 1810 and the final printed version of 1857 and will focus on (1) the embellishment of the text; (2) the introduction of Christian motifs; (3) the representation of social reality; and (4) the erasure of the mother and the depiction of the witch.

Embellishment of the Text

After the publication of the first edition of 1812–1815, the Grimms were advised by various friends to alter the style of the tales and to try to address young readers instead of scholars if they wanted their book to become more popular. In fact, all of Wilhelm's efforts from 1819 onward were directed toward improving the texts by creating greater clarity, transition, rationalization, and description to heighten their appeal to reading audiences. Moreover, he omitted many tales because of their vulgarity, and with his great knowledge of different versions, he kept combining them and adapting motifs to make the tales suitable for a popular market. In the case of "Hansel and Gretel," Wilhelm embellished the rough, terse written manuscript of 1810 in many different ways. By introducing direct speech, he deepened the characterization of the father and step-mother so that he becomes much more caring and concerned about the children and she becomes more coldhearted and cruel. In fact, she is demonstrably the evil agent and calls her husband a fool and the children "lazybones," while he is worried about the "poor" chil-dren. Throughout the text, Wilhelm added numerous diminutives to make the story more charming as well as descriptive words and explanations so that the actions of all the characters would become more rationally based. For instance, instead of the one line that introduces the old woman in the Ölenberg manuscript, we have:

> The old woman, however, had only pretended to be friendly. She was really a wicked witch on the lookout for children, and had built the house made of bread only to lure them to her. As soon as she had any children in her power, she would kill, cook, and eat them. It would be like a feast day for her. Now, witches have red eyes and cannot see very far, but they have a keen sense of smell, like ani-mals, and can detect when human beings are near them. Therefore, when Hansel and Gretel had come into her vicinity, she had laughed wickedly and scoffed, "They're mine! They'll never get away from me!"[8]

Such embellishments were added not simply to make the tale more exciting and dramatic but to create more order and to base the motivations of the characters on the ideological perspective of the Brothers Grimm—what Germans often refer to as a *Weltan-schauung*. In this particular case, the "evil" in the tale is shifted from the bad actions of a father and stepmother to a female witch, the opposite of the male Christian God. From this point on in the story, the quest of the two children is not just to survive abandon-ment but to overcome abuse in the form of the witch.

The embellishments in the tale were also used to soften the sense of abandonment and abuse; that is, words and incidents sweeten the text so that it becomes more quaint and provides comfort to readers. Consequently, a beautiful white bird with a lovely voice leads the children to the witch's house so they can have a blessed meal of milk, pancakes, apples, and nuts. Later, after Gretel has pushed the witch into the oven, we are told that "Hansel jumped out of the pen like a bird that hops out of a cage when the door is opened. My, how happy they were! They hugged each other, danced around, and kissed."[9] And of course, there is the cute little duck that carries them safely to their father, who—an addition—"had not had a single happy hour since he had abandoned his children in the forest."[10]

The Introduction of Christian Motifs

Aside from bringing about more rational order in the tale, Wilhelm also added Christian motifs to the printed versions of "Hansel and Gretel," something that he did with many other tales as well. In this case, there are three important incidents in which the children call upon God to help them. The first two times, Hansel consoles the frightened Gretel when they are still at home by saying, "Just sleep in peace. God will not forsake us" and "The dear Lord is bound to help us." Later, when Gretel is ordered to help the witch to cook Hansel, she exclaims, "Dear God, help us!" These references to God are not just common expressions; they transform the anonymous "pagan" children of the Ölenberg manuscript into good, Christian, God-fearing children. It is thus their "goodness" and faith in God that enable them to overcome the evil witch. Moreover, abandoned by one father, they must appeal to another, divine father, who will not desert them. Fathers are continually extolled in the tale, whether they be biological or divine.

The Representation of Social Reality

In all the literary versions of the "Hansel and Gretel"–type tale from Basile through Perrault, it is clear that the parents are poor and starving and are more or less driven to abandon their children. Yet none of these versions is as clear as Wilhelm's text in depicting the social background. Twice he refers to a great famine that was devastating the entire country, and in fact, there were many famines in the period between 1810 and 1857 that caused great misery for the peasantry in Hesse and in central Europe. Sensitive to the problems of the peasantry, Wilhelm stressed the need for bread, for a simple meal. When Hansel and Gretel discover the witch's house, it is made largely of bread, not gingerbread. The theme of nourishment is a crucial metaphorical aspect of this tale. Spiritually, psychologically, and physically the children are deprived of nourishment. Their condition, though extreme, was representative of that of numerous peasant households in Germany during the first half of the nineteenth century, especially during famines. In this regard, the Grimms' fairy tale sheds light on social realities of the times in a manner that many didactic and so-called realistic tales of this period concealed.

The Erasure of the Mother and the Depiction of the Witch

One of the major changes made by Wilhelm was to cast the biological mother as a stepmother in the second edition of 1819. In addition, he also suggested that the stepmother may be associated with the witch, leading to a demonization of women in the tale. For instance, the stepmother wakes the children and calls them "lazybones," just as the witch later wakes Gretel and calls her "lazybones." In addition, both are duplicitous, appearing friendly while seeking to destroy the children. It is difficult to say why Wilhelm erased the biological mother from the text. Is it possible that because he and Jacob revered their own mother, they did not want to depict a biological mother abandoning her own children? Or was Wilhelm convinced that it would make more sense, as in Basile's tale "Ninnillo and Nennella," to portray a stepmother who resented looking after and nourishing children who were not her own? Certainly, given the fact that many women died in childbirth in the eighteenth and nineteenth centuries, numerous men, left with motherless children, remarried and brought stepmothers into their homes. Though not all stepmothers were threats to their stepchildren, they would likely be more interested in starting their own families and looking after their own children, if they had any, than in caring for their stepchildren. By replacing the biological mother with the stepmother, Wilhelm may again have wanted to represent social realities of his time. Yet, whatever his motive, neither step-mother nor witch is given any saving features. They are both self-centered and want to destroy the children. The stepmother could not care less if wild animals eat the children in the woods. She wants to get rid of them, to eradicate them from her life. The witch is a predator, an ogress, who wants to eat them. In the end, both evil women are killed in the text by Wilhelm in the name of goodness and God.

This is not to say that Wilhelm was a misogynist or that he had nefarious reasons for depicting women as he did in "Hansel and Gretel." Nor did he have any sinister purposes in making the changes in the tale. Yet how do we explain the major changes? What were the underlying causes? The most obvious, as I have already stated, is the Grimms' design of presenting popular tales in a form that would effectively leave an impression on their readers that each tale represented a German cultural heritage that held the people together as one large family. Therefore, if there were lapses or non sequiturs, or incidents that needed explication in their collected stories, then the Grimms, mainly Wilhelm, kept rewriting the tales to guarantee that there would be smooth transitions, logical development of the plots, and appropriate characterization that would meet the expectations of their readers and their own standards of artistic style and scholarly research. By 1857 Wilhelm had finely honed and ordered each tale. In "Hansel and Gretel," Wilhelm went to great pains to explain and demonstrate why the abandonment of the children had to take place and why the father should be exculpated in the end. Aberrant actions are made rational, but in the process there is a rationalization of the father's deed that reinforces a patriarchal social and symbolical order. In the rational structure of the text, abuse takes place on two levels: The children, Hansel and Gretel, are abused by having nourishment withheld from them and eventually are drawn into accepting the rule of the father as more benevolent than that of the mother; and children as young readers are abused by following the rational order of the text and being misled to conceive that order will always be restored through the intervention of God the father and a resolution that restores faith in the good father. In each case, there is a particular kind of abusive "domestication of the imagination" that Rüdiger Steinlein notes became common in much German children's literature at the beginning of the nineteenth century.[11] By "domestication of the imagination," Steinlein means that the narrative strategies of stories, particularly fairy tales, became ordered in such a way that children would become reconciled to the hierarchical structures in their daily lives and accept social arrangements as authoritative and just, particularly as they existed in the middle-class families at that time, where most readers were to be found. In Steinlein's most recent study of the Grimms' tales,[12] he stresses the fact that the *Kinder- und Hausmärchen* was conceived as an *Erziehungsbuch* (educational book), and through Wilhelm's elaborate process of rewriting and reconceptualizing the tales, the pedagogical elements were poeticized through a shift from the authoritative male voice to the soft voice of the nurturing mother, who was now playing a key role in the socialization of children in middle-class families in Germany. According to Steinlein, Wilhelm Grimm's achievement consisted of his ability to harmonize the plot and action of the fairy tales with the norms and expectations of the bourgeois reading public at that time. Wilhelm cultivated a poetic style that produced a comforting tone, awakened a specific desire for maternal connection and home, and created an atmosphere of trust. This tone expresses the ideal of nuclear-familial relations as intimate discourse (speech), and it may act as an expanded organ of the familial in that it temporarily harmonizes or balances the strange and threatening contradictions of social reality through the mythical-magical events and humor of the fairy tale while at the same time imparting proper ways to behave and think. The result is that the imagination of readers undergoes a kind of domestication that does not *seem* to be harmful, pedagogical, or manipulative because of the coded maternal tone.

In "Hansel and Gretel" Wilhelm Grimm's poetics of domestication and pedagogy are clearly manifested through his rewriting: the choice of words and phrases and the rearrangement of the plot.

Lurking behind the very first word is a notion of ideal domesticity that the voice of the narrative will eventually convey more carefully. The children are moved from the breakdown of order in a domestic situation, caused by a woman, to another threatening domestic situation, in which the woman again represents the forces of chaos and destruction. Though the children are actually saved by their own wits, it is implied that they are saved by God's grace. Fearful of the forest or of living independently, they are ultimately redomesticated and place their riches at the disposal of their father as sole ruler of the house. Children as readers or listeners are prompted to follow each step that the brother-sister pair take and are stimulated to believe that the ordered design of the tale leads to happiness. But the liberation from the evil witch is not a liberation of their imagination. They are not to think autonomously or to separate themselves from the symbolic order of the father. Instead, as readers they are encouraged to identify with Hansel and Gretel, who end by helping to reestablish the order and power of the father.

As Wilhelm kept reordering the tale, he set an exemplary mode for the literary appropriation of oral tales in the nineteenth century, and his work poses many problems for interpretation especially if one wants to explore the psychosocial aspects of the tale and the way we have continued to receive it in Western societies. I want to consider two significant approaches that do not lead to definitive answers but open up perspectives on the tale that have rarely been explored: (1) an interpretation of the tale as Wilhelm's artwork; and (2) an analysis of the tale's sociopsychological ramifications in contemporary society in relation to the rationalization of child abandonment and the domestication of the imagination.

Wilhelm's literary appropriation of Dortchen Wild's oral tale was an act of preservation and at the same time an act of rhetorical violence. By writing down Dortchen's words, he saved them for posterity and contributed to our understanding of an oral tradition. Yet as he began to change and manipulate her words, he violated her intent and desire; her words became his, and even the title, invented by his brother, indicated that her signature on the tale would be effaced. As far as we know, Wilhelm wrote from memory.

That is, he did not take shorthand or sit in front of Dortchen Wild and inscribe her words one by one. He heard and absorbed her words and tried to retain in memory the sense of her story. But once he wrote down the tale and then rewrote it, the narrative strategy became an enactment of his desires, drives, and intent.

If we accept that the plot and style of his different "Hansel and Gretel" versions were governed by Wilhelm's unconscious drives, aesthetic taste, and ideological perspective, then various questions arise that may shed light on why the tale eventually assumed the form and meaning that it did. I have already remarked that Wilhelm and Jacob loved their mother a great deal, and that one of the reasons the biological mother became a stepmother may be attributable to Wilhelm's reluctance to portray a wicked mother figure. There are other biographical factors that may have played a role in Wilhelm's rewritings of the tale. When Wilhelm was nine years old, he and Jacob lost their father, and the brothers vowed never to separate. In fact, they never did. On a certain level, it is possible to assume that Hansel and Gretel form an androgynous pair, a loving couple, representative of the brothers. There are indications in the Grimms' autobiographical writings and letters that they felt abandoned and were compelled to shift for themselves as best they could. Psychologically, the reunion with the father in this tale may have been an act of forgiveness or of wish-fulfillment. Even the effacement of the mother/stepmother could mean that Wilhelm unconsciously blamed their mother for forcing their father to abandon them. Was he unconsciously punishing her for pushing their father to commit a crime? The brothers did experience some sort of trauma after their father's death that was quickly repressed. Sent to Kassel as poor students, they were isolated and left on their own at an early age. Evil was the destruction of domestic tranquility, the continual threat of separation and poverty, and not earning enough bread for the large family—and evil also took the form of the invasion of Kassel by the French during the Napoleonic Wars (1805–1812) and of the king of Hannover, who had the brothers driven out of Göttingen in 1837.

Wilhelm and Jacob were God-fearing, studious, and sincere, and throughout their lives they desired a secure domestic situation that would enable them to pursue their studies. They also wished for a state that would be ruled according to the dictates of reason, a constitutional monarchy in which voices of reason would be heard. The movement in "Hansel and Gretel" resembles a movement away from domestic insecurity to a state of terror (the house of the witch) and back to a reconstituted home, in which the authority is a benevolent, caring father. Evil in the form of a selfish, ruthless stepmother and a cannibalistic witch is expunged. There is no more chaos. Compassion and reason constitute happiness at the end of the tale as scripted by Wilhelm.

If the tale embodies Wilhelm's unconscious fears and desires, it also represents his ideas and knowledge that he wanted to impart to his readers. He consciously and purposely introduced ideas about the family, child rearing, and social conditions to instruct and to explain the reasons behind the narrative's incidents. For instance, as I have already remarked, he was keenly aware of the sufferings of the peasants during the famine years in the nineteenth century, and he apparently wanted to reflect on how a famine could drive poor people to desperation. Here it also becomes apparent why the mother/stepmother might want to get rid of the children more than the father does. Shulamith Shahar points out that in the late Middle Ages, although legislators and authors of didactic works did not recommend allocating less food to women than to men, "poorer families, particularly at times of famine, appear to have apportioned the meager food supplies in their possession to the husband and children. Many more women than men in the lower classes were afflicted with blindness and various bone malformations as a result of malnutrition. Temporary infertility in women in the labouring classes was apparently sometimes caused by the cessation of menses due to starvation (famine amenorrhoea). This phenomenon of self-deprivation on the part of the mother which is accepted by the family is familiar today also in some countries in the Third World."[13]

If the stepmother in "Hansel and Gretel" is expected, as a good mother might be, to give up her life for her husband and stepchildren during a famine, it becomes more understandable that Wilhelm should depict her as insisting more than the husband on getting rid of the children. Here is a woman who does not believe in self-deprivation, especially when the children are not her own. The abandonment of the children is less a crime than her desire (and her husband's complicity is important) to survive the famine. This "unchristian" act is then associated with the devil, and Wilhelm's introduction of a paragraph of folklore about witches followed the general belief in Germany that witches ate children and were associated with women, chaos, and destruction. From Wilhelm's perspective, men were superior to women and represented the principles of reason and logos. Therefore, the triumph over the witch could occur only through faith and trust in God, who leads the children back to the proper governing father, who had neglected his duties but is now ready to supervise the rearing of the children by himself.

"Hansel and Gretel" is very much a didactic Christian story. *There is nothing really magical* in the tale, with the exception of the house and the duck, when one considers that at that time people believed witches really existed. It is a narrative about the abandonment of children that Wilhelm arranged according to his own lines of thinking and desire. As a finely crafted tale, each word and phrase were carefully weighed and elaborated after the initial writing of 1810. Like some of the other tales in the Grimms' collection, it has been a favorite of readers throughout Western societies and, as I have mentioned, has become a classic, though that was not necessarily Wilhelm's choice or intent. Therefore, it is important to ask why we have honored the tale the way we have during the past 150 years and what the possible consequences are for children.

Since Böhm-Korff has done a comprehensive study of the manner in which the tale has been interpreted and used in Germany since its origins, it is not necessary to repeat her summaries of the different approaches. But it is necessary to expand and elaborate on her work because she does not deal with the reception of the tale in other cultures, and she arrives at a cautious conclusion that, I believe, limits her work. Admitting that the tale can legitimately be interpreted in many different ways, she believes that the historical focus of the tale on abandonment should be the primary starting point for grasping its key meaning. However, I should like to be less cautious, go one step further than Böhm-Korff, and insist upon a historical focus not simply on abandonment but on the rationalization of abandonment and the domestication of the imagination.

One of the difficulties in discussing the reception of a tale like "Hansel and Gretel" and its sociopsychological ramifications is that every culture has its own unique history of adapting, receiving, disseminating, discussing, debating, and using a classical fairy tale. Moreover, each time a tale is read, heard, or seen, the receiver will project conscious and unconscious feelings onto it on an individual level. Nor can we know whether the receiver has even encountered the 1857 version of "Hansel and Gretel." For instance, in Germany Engelbert Humperdinck's opera *Hänsel und Gretel* (1893) has had a profound influence on the manner in which the Grimms' tale is visualized and read in Germany, and many popular editions of the tale have been changed to accord with the libretto written by Humperdinck's sister, Adelheid Wette.[14] Not only did Wette transform the Grimms' stepmother into the biological mother; she also made both parents sympathetic and turned the tale into a kind of Christian parable, celebrating God the Father's majesty and benevolence. At the end of the opera, the mother and father go searching for the children and find them at the witch's house.

MOTHER: Children!
FATHER: There they are, the little sinners! (Joyful reunion. Meanwhile two boys drag the witch in the form of a large gingerbread figure out of the ruins of the magic oven. Upon sight of her everyone begins to rejoice. The boys place the witch in the middle of the stage.)
FATHER: Children, look at this miraculous sight,
              How the witch has lost her might,
              how hard,
              crispy hard
              she herself is now a cake.
              See how Heaven's judgment works:
              Evil deeds do not last!
              When our need is at its most,
              The Lord our God gives us a helping hand!

EVERYONE: When our need is at its most,
The lord our God gives us a helping hand![15]

In Wette's "Hansel and Gretel," the children are made into "little sinners" because they have broken something in the house and are sent out into the woods to look for strawberries. They wander about and get lost. In other words, Wette shifts the blame for the abandonment onto the children themselves, and she effaces any hint of child abuse and abandonment. Her line of reasoning is the fulfillment of the rationalization of child abuse that can be traced to the Grimms' tale itself and is part of a "rationalist aesthetics" characteristic of Charles Perrault's tales.

What Wette did, of course, was not a crime but was in keeping with a traditional reception of fairy tales that reflects the concerns of dominant ideological forces, conditions in the culture industry, and social and cultural beliefs. It is well known that "Hansel and Gretel" has been translated and adapted hundreds if not thousands of times throughout the world, and writers and publishers have taken many liberties with it. Indeed, some educators and parents have objected to Gretel's pushing the witch into an oven and have placed pressure on publishers to eliminate this episode. At the end of World War II, some so-called authorities among the Allied Forces of Occupation thought that the cruelty and sadism in the Grimms' fairy tales had contributed to Nazism, and the oven scene in "Hansel and Gretel" was particularly disturbing for many readers after 1945.

There is no doubt that particular scenes, symbols, or motifs can cause a traumatic or highly affective reaction in a reader, and here it is perhaps a therapist's role to consider why, or it is the reader's own task to reflect upon why he or she has such a strong emotional response to a given fairy tale. Yet I believe that despite the vast number of possible responses to "Hansel and Gretel" and the validity of these responses, and despite the different cultural traditions and historical shifts in the reception of this tale, there may be a common denominator to explain why the tale has become so popular in Western societies.

As we know, though it may be difficult to make demographic comparisons with Western societies of the eighteenth, nineteenth, and early twentieth centuries, child abuse in the form of battering, abandonment, sexual violation, psychological manipulation, discarding, and killing unfortunately has not abated during the second half of the twentieth century. If anything, in America it seems to have increased, and child abuse does not occur in just one social class. In fact, I would argue in agreement with the psychoanalyst Alice Miller that every child encounters some form of abuse and grows up fearing abuse and abandonment.[16] The actual experience with abuse and the fear of abandonment is a matter of degree, and once we reach adulthood, we want to minimize this degree as well as our complicity in such abuse.

In my opinion, "Hansel and Gretel" has always minimized and will continue to minimize that degree in all societies. It is a soothing, pacifying tale that touches on issues of abuse and abandonment and provides hope that security and happiness can be found after a traumatic episode. It empathizes with the children and with the father in a hopeful conclusion that allows for reconciliation and reunion. But I fear that it is also a tale that reinforces male hegemony and exculpates men from a crime against children, or that rationalizes the manner in which men use the bonds of love to reinforce their control over children.

If we reexamine the paradigmatic object relations in the tale, it is fascinating to see how it is structured to focus on the overcoming of abandonment and on celebrating the Oedipus complex and the power of the male in the return home to the father. Psychologically speaking, the two children feel threatened by a mother figure, who is demonized twice in the tale. She is the one who really wants to cast them out and the one who wants to eat them. It is in flight from the smothering, omnipotent mother that the children seek solace and security in a father, who becomes their ultimate authority figure when the mother is erased from their lives. The object relations within the tale for the most part reflect the manner in which object relations have been arranged in Western societies up to the present. In other words, as Jessica Benjamin has pointed out in *The Bonds of Love*, the mother figure is the dominant nurturer during the first two years of a child's life and is both a positive and a negative figure, certainly daunting and omnipotent. Out of fear of this omnipotence, the child turns to male power for help.

This turn toward the male, however, is a concession and will enable the male authority to dictate the child's life on his terms. Once the male has the child in his power, he can be benevolent or sadistic; it does not matter, but he is in control, and it seems *reasonable* that he remain in control.

Not by chance have the paradigmatic object relations within "Hansel and Gretel" been continually accepted and played out in the minds of readers and writers in the manner that I have suggested. As John Boswell states in his important study *The Kindness of Strangers: The Abandonment of Children in Western Europe from Late Antiquity to the Renaissance*, "abandonment is such a regular fulcrum for plots in ancient literature, moreover, that it is somewhat difficult to imagine its effectiveness if it were not part of the experience of much of the audience."[17] In fact, abandonment is a major motif in literature up to the present, just as it has in some form been part of the experience of most people up to the present, and it is generally associated with abuse in some form or another. What is significant, however, is not so much the representation of abandonment but the *joyous* overcoming of abandonment and reconciliation with the parents or abusers. Boswell is again enlightening on this point: "The happiest but least convincing outcome of abandonment in literary treatments is the ecstatic recovery of children by natal parents (or vice versa). Beginning with Oedipus, exposed children in literature set out to find their parents, and their parents to reclaim their offspring, and under the benevolent reign of kindly authors clement circumstances conspire to make this *anagnorsis*, as ancient writers called it, come to pass."[18] Then Boswell raises some important questions about the happy endings to abandonment:

> Are such scenes realistic? That such happy endings were useful for the writers is a moot point. They may, of course, have distorted the likelihood of parental recovery to achieve dramatic ends, or emphasized a delightful but remote possibility. If so, it is revealing that of many possible resolutions of plot available to them storytellers chose this one. Perhaps a public that included a good many parents who had exposed children yearned for such a consummation, or even expected it, in the way that modern audiences expect love

affairs to end happily, not because in life they always do, but because they sometimes do, and one wishes they always would.[19]

Given the fact that from early antiquity to the present, abandonment has been accepted as a "sensible" if not legal mode of dealing with children when *they* become problems, this abusive form of treating children needed, in my opinion, some form of justification, legitimation, and apology in the minds of parents. Or it needed many forms because the modes of abandonment and attitudes toward them kept changing. Yet, as Boswell hints, adults have always felt uncomfortable about abandonment even while practicing it with apparent equanimity. Therefore, the happy ending or recovery serves an ideological function, making it appear that parents are not guilty—*they* are not the problem. At least, in the case of "Hansel and Gretel," the father is not the problem.

Politically, states and families in Western societies have been based on male hierarchical rule, and fairy tales, which have played such an important part in the socialization of children, contain arrangements that lend credence to power structures and legitimate the power of adults. Therefore, to be truly accepted as a classical fairy tale and presumed "good" for the well-being of children, a narrative must be eminently rational and subscribe to notions of the acceptable treatment of children and male hegemony, even if the structure of the tale conceals and perhaps perpetuates abuse of children. Otherwise, it will not become classical or popular. "Hansel and Gretel" is both classical and popular.

3

Toward a Theory
of the Fairy-Tale Film

The Case of Pinocchio

Animation should be an art, that is how I conceived it ... but as I
see what you fellows have done with it is making it into a trade ...
not an art, but a trade ... *bad luck.*
        —Winsor McCay, addressing young animators in 1927

Just as we know—almost intuitively—that a particular narrative
is a fairy tale when we read it, we seem to know immediately that
a particular film is a fairy tale when we see it. We recognize its
generic qualities without necessarily interpreting it as part of a
genre. It is almost as though it were natural for fairy-tale films to
exist because fairy tales are so much a part of our cultural heritage
as oral and literary tales. However, this "natural" process of recognition and consumption makes it all the more important that we
examine the history of the fairy-tale film to understand what has
gone into its making. When did it come about? Why? What are the
consequences? Of course, these questions cannot all be answered
within a short chapter, but by using Walt Disney's adaptation of
Carlo Collodi's fairy-tale novel *Pinocchio*, I want to suggest possible
approaches toward developing a theory of the fairy-tale film as
genre. First, however, I shall present five brief theses about the
development of the fairy tale as film.

Pinnocchio, illustrated by Charles Folkard, from Carlo Collodi, *Pinnocchio* (London: J. M. Dent, 1911)

1. As we know, storytelling is thousands of years old, and there are many types of tales. In the oral tradition, the "magic tale" generally centered on a miraculous transformation or occurrence that enabled the protagonist to triumph over evil forces or overcome obstacles to win a bride or groom, obtain wealth, or gain recognition within a tribe or community. The oral tales were told in many different settings—in all sorts of tribes and communities, in homes, at taverns, in the fields, at sea, in weaving circles, and so on. No matter what the situation, the teller was present and in person among a group of people and told tales to share experience, to amuse, and to enlighten the listeners. (Of course, this kind of storytelling still occurs.) Most important, storytelling created a bond between teller and listeners and often reflected customs, norms, and values within the group. Since one had to be artful in the telling of tales, and since most people were not particularly "artful" or articulate in days of old, as Rudolph Schenda has maintained,[1] the taleteller was highly regarded within a community. Telling tales, using words and symbols, endowed the speaker with authority and power. A magic folk tale concerned not only the miraculous turn of events in the story but also the magical play of words by the teller as performer, and each performance by the same teller was different. Tales could be told over and over again in new ways. The close personal setting affected all concerned. Storytelling is fluid, alive, and unpredictable and can be altered to fit any setting. The taleteller changes in the telling of the story and shifts his or her identity like the remarkable trickster of the folk-tale tradition. Telling a magic folk tale was and is not unlike performing a magic trick, and depending on the art of the storyteller, listeners are placed under a spell. They are in awe, and to be in awe is to be in a special place, linked with the teller and other members of the group, transcending reality for a brief moment, to be transported to extraordinary regions of experience.

2.   There is evidence of magic folk tales in all the sacred literature of the world. That is, the motifs of magic folk tales were incorporated into all of the early texts, such as the Bible, *The Iliad*, and *The Odyssey*, concerned with the origins of gods and with initiation rituals. Another early classical example in the West is Apuleius's *The Golden Ass*, in which we find the complete magical tale of Cupid and Psyche. However, one cannot speak of the literary fairy tale as genre until after the invention of the printing press, the growth of literacy and vernacular languages, and the establishment of genres as institutions, which means examining this literary form in light of its production, reception, and distribution. A literary genre could not flower in Europe during the Renaissance until it became socially acceptable, that is, instituted within a social practice that furthered its production, reception, and distribution. As institution, a literary genre is tied to the socioeconomic and cultural context of a society or state. Chaucer and Boccaccio prepared the way for the fairy tale, but the formative signs of a literary genre can first be found in Giovan Francesco Straparola's *Le Piacevoli Notti* (*Pleasant Nights*, 1550–1553) and Giambattista Basile's *Lo Cunto de li Cunti*, better known as *Il Pentamerone* (1634–1636). As literature, the fairy tale became reading matter, and as such, it was cultivated mainly for the educated classes and became more complex in theme and structure. The Italian and French fairy tales of the sixteenth and seventeenth centuries are long, sophisticated symbolical narratives that address issues of decorum and behavior within the European civilizing process and questions of power between classes and sexes. Though often read aloud, they were produced for private absorption and circulated largely among members of the upper classes. They represented the views of particular authors who pretended they were universal tales. To the extent that authors such as Straparola, Basile, Perrault, Mme. D'Aulnoy, Mlle. L'Héritier, and others appropriated the

tales from an oral tradition, they incorporated motifs, characters, and plots from folk culture. But it is important to remember that literary fairy tales were feudal artworks. That is, they represented the concerns of aristocratic or middle-class authors and were directed at a select group of adult readers, generally those who were part of court or salon society. This definition does not mean that the early literary fairy tales legitimized absolutism, but it does mean that the power plays among kings, queens, princes, princesses, monsters, and fairies were understood as commentaries on normative behavior and the use of power in the existing sixteenth- and seventeenth-century hierarchical societies. The fairy tales served a dual social function in representing the power invested in aristocratic elites: They were a mode of entertainment through which the upper classes could take delight in their own machinations, but they were also symbolically subversive, for they were secular instructive narratives, strategies of intervention within the civilizing process that often revealed abuses of power and authority. It was during this time that the fairy tale as institutionalized genre began to flower and expand as ballet, opera, and court festival.

3. After the fairy tale became institutionalized in France during the 1790s, it became free, so to speak, to expand its form and content. As the demographics of the reading public and the means of production changed in the eighteenth and nineteenth centuries, so did the fairy tale. What had once been exclusively reading matter for adults was transformed in part into reading matter for children. Mme. Le Prince de Beaumont's *Magasin des enfants* (1756) used approximately ten fairy tales, including "Beauty and the Beast," to instruct young girls in how to domesticate themselves and become respectable young women, attractive for the marriage market. By the beginning of the nineteenth century there were four broad currents in the development of the fairy tale as genre:

(a) The oral tradition was enriched by the incorporation of literary tales that were transformed by their listeners and readers, and new kinds of oral tales were developed by talented storytellers whose narratives often returned to influence the literary tradition; (b) literary fairy tales with illustrations were published for children, and the content and structure of the tales were made more appropriate to what educators and governing bodies within bourgeois institutions deemed suitable for children; (c) literary fairy tales for adults became a highly sophisticated genre and expanded their audience so that different types of tales, some with a strong political content and others as *l'art pour l'art* were produced by the end of the nineteenth century and beginning of the twentieth; (d) the fairy tale served as the structural and thematic determinant for operas, plays, ballets, poems, musicals, and advertisements that became part of the genre as institution.

Most significant in all these currents was that the identifiable voice of the storyteller who was part of a community had shifted to the literary voice, with a narrator no longer present and not clearly identifiable, and by the nineteenth century this voice assumed a paternal role. Though it has often been argued that the fairy tale was part of a female domain, this idea is not true. At least, it is not true of the literary fairy tale. By the end of the nineteenth century, the major writers of the fairy tale were mostly men—the Brothers Grimm, Wilhelm Hauff, Ludwig Bechstein, Hans Christian Andersen, Carl Ewald, William Makepeace Thackeray, George Mac-Donald, Lewis Carroll, Oscar Wilde, Andrew Lang, Joseph Jacobs, Carlo Collodi, Frank Stockton, and L. Frank Baum—as were most of the collectors. They were responsible—and so were many women writers—for a kind of "family fairy tale"; that is, their tales addressed the entire family, and notions such as industry, diligence, justice, and achievement became more prominent in their tales than aristocratic majesty and absolute power. In fact, the fairy tale was no longer a feudal artwork, but had become autonomous. In a free market system, it came to be packaged as a household good (remember that the Grimms called their collection *Children's and Household Tales*), and the family fairy tale as commodity was designed to reinforce patriarchal notions of civilization, whether it was produced by male or female authors. Most fairy tales were not didactic, but as a genre the fairy tale was clearly recognized as *the discourse* for the entire family in which questions of proper gender behavior, the treatment of children, the employment of power, standards of success, norms, and values could be presented and debated.

4. By the beginning of the twentieth century, the fairy tale in most of its forms had become family fare, and it is not by chance that the French pioneer filmmaker Georges Méliès began experimenting as early as 1896 with types of fantasy and fairy-tale motifs in his *féeries,* or trick films. In fact he produced well over a hundred short silent films and often used fairy tales such as "Cinderella," "Bluebeard," "Little Red Riding Hood," and "Sleeping Beauty" to project magical worlds that, to a great extent, celebrated the powers of the filmmaker as magician. As Gerald Mast has remarked, "the Méliès films owe their superiority to the wild imagination and subtle debunking humor of their master. Méliès was by trade a magician; just as earlier magicians had adopted the magic lantern, Méliès adopted moving pictures. He saw the camera's ability to stop and start again brought the magician's two greatest arts to perfection—disappearance and conversion; anything could be converted into anything else; anything could vanish."[2] The fairy-tale work of Méliès and animation in general were preceded by many nineteenth-century experiments that incorporated or made use of fairy tales. In *Enchanted Drawings: The History of Animation,* Charles Solomon has described how magic

lantern shows, magician's tricks, shadow theaters, animation devices, and sequential photography contributed to the making of motion pictures and led such early pioneers as James Stuart Blackton, Emile Cohl, Winsor McCay, and Méliès to introduce all kinds of traditional and original fairy-tale motifs into their films. By far the most innovative of the early fairy-tale animators was McCay, who created *Little Nemo in Slumberland* in 1905 as a cartoon and later transformed it into an animated film. Not only did he conceive unique fairy-tale and fantasy films with new plots such as *Little Nemo* (1911), *How a Mosquito Operates* (1912), and *Gertie the Dinosaur* (1914), he also introduced artistic techniques to make characters move smoothly and realistically and paid great attention to color and character development. However, McCay, like all animators during the first three decades of the twentieth century, was more concerned with technique than content. A main purpose of these animators' work was to impress audiences with their technical inventions, to create a spectacle, and often this aim involved what Donald Crafton has called self-figuration:

> The early animated film was the location of a process found elsewhere in cinema but nowhere else in such intense concentration: self-figuration, the tendency of the filmmaker to interject himself into his film. This can take several forms, it can be direct or indirect, and more or less camouflaged.... At first it was obvious and literal; at the end it was subtle and cloaked in metaphors and symbolic imagery designed to facilitate the process and yet to keep the idea gratifying for the artist and the audience. Part of the animation game consisted of developing mythologies that gave the animator some sort of special status. Usually these were very flattering, for he was pictured as (or implied to be) a demigod, a purveyor of life itself.[3]

Most of the fairy-tale films of the early twentieth-century had flimsy story lines and little character development. The emphasis was placed on the gag, action (cat-and-mouse episodes), and invention so that the filmmaker could display his technical ability to produce calculated effects that were to make audiences sit in awe. For the fairy tale as a genre, the introduction of animation and motion picture films led to the following developments:

a. Image dominated text. Since early animation was without sound, the tales were voiceless. Whatever text appeared was minimal. Though one-dimensional, the images of the characters—as in illustrated books— were projected by the producers to the audiences.

b. In the fairy-tale film, the major protagonist was no longer the character but the filmmaker as magician behind the scenes.

c. The appropriation of traditional fairy tales and the creation of new fairy tales through film created even further distance from the storyteller (the producers of the film) and the audience.

d. As the fairy tale was "standardized" so that it could transcend particular communities and interests, it structurally fit into the economic mode of production known during that time as Taylorism or Fordism. Films were intended to be mass produced as commodities in a rational process based on cost efficiency, and their major design was for profit.

In short, the fairy-tale film silenced the personal and communal voice of the oral magic tales and obfuscated the personal voice of literary fairy-tale narratives. Through the images and gradually through sound, all voices were leveled in the name of an administrative or industrialized voice that narrated in fairy tales in seemingly authentic tones and yet effaced any particular impulses and features connected to the oral and literary tradition. The "new" communal voice was standardized and bent on selling itself in the form of a commodified fairy tale. What pleasure and meaning audiences were to derive from the cinematic fairy tale was incidental to the purpose of the producers.

5.   By the 1930s there was a major shift in the film industry, thanks to the introduction of sound and color and numerous other technological devices. These developments enabled filmmakers to contemplate greater projects with the fairy tale. Already in 1917 the Argentinean filmmaker Quirino Crisitiani had produced a feature-length animated film titled *The Apostle*, and Lotte Reiniger had finished her silhouette feature, *The Adventures of Prince Ahmed*, in Germany in 1926. Raoul Walsh had produced one of the first live-action fairy-tale films, *The Thief of Baghdad* (1924), with Douglas Fairbanks. Though it is unclear whether Walt Disney and his animators knew about these films, he had been preparing for the production of full-length animated films since the 1920s and had already made several fascinating fairy-tale films in 1922 and 1923 with Ub Iwerks in Kansas City.[4] Therefore, with improved technology, it was a logical step for Disney and other filmmakers to adapt fairy tales for feature-length films. Disney completed *Snow White and the Seven Dwarfs* in 1937 and *Pinocchio* in 1940. MGM produced *The Wonderful Wizard of Oz* in 1939; Ernst Lubitsch produced *Ball of Fire* with Jimmy Stewart in 1941; and Jean Cocteau's first film after World War II was *Beauty and the Beast* (1946). Indeed, ever since World War II the fairy tale as live-action film or animation has become one of the most successful genres in the culture industry. Perhaps, given the barbarism of World War II, the need for fairy tales in the mass media became greater afterward, for it is through the fairy tale that hope for happy endings is kept alive. The question we must ask, however, is whether it is a false hope. Do fairy-tale films project false utopias through amusement? Have fairy-tale films contributed to the destruction of community and the deception of the masses?

Though there are many types of fairy-tale films, Disney's work in the 1930s certainly set the model for most of the animated fairy-tale films that were to be produced in the later twentieth century. Some of the key elements of his work with fairy tales follow:

a. Given the rationalization of the production process that he established in his studios, the story line was developed through the collective work of the animators, with Disney having the last word. Since all of the animators were male, the ideas, gags, and themes emanated from a kind of boys' locker-room talk. There was often an infantile type of humor in the early Disney films, resembling the pranks boys are prone to play.[5]

b. The classical tale was reshaped to suit the basic format of the musical and the adventure tale. The structure involved the introduction of the major protagonist, who soon gets into trouble and must be rescued or must rescue himself, depending on the sex. Females do not rescue themselves in Disney films, but they do sing. The simple story is punctuated with comic relief (generally animals, strange little people, or foppish characters) and song.

c. Since the story line was so simplistic and familiar, the technical artistry and invention were highlighted to command the audience's attention.

d. In traditional fairy tales that Disney adapted for the screen, there were very few major plot changes because Disney and his coworkers generally subscribed to the ideological content of the action. In this respect, Disney depicted clear-cut gender roles that associated women with domesticity and men with action and power. Evil characters are inevitably dark or black, while the protagonists are fair.

e. The fairy-tale film was the centerpiece of a package that consisted of various commodities attached to it:

a program, an illustrated book, a doll, a poster, a ceramic model, a piece of clothing. Today the package is even larger.

f. As commodity, the fairy-tale film sacrificed art to technical invention; innovation to tradition; stimulation of the imagination to consumption for distraction.

Though it is clear that the Disney model—even within the Disney corporation itself—has given way in the latter part of the twentieth century to more experimental fairy-tale films, both animated and live-action, this model remains a dominant force. One need only look at more recent fairy-tale films such as the "feminist" *Happily Ever After* (1993), or even Disney's *Beauty and the Beast* (1993) and *The Lion King* (1994), or Shelley Duvall's video series *Faerie Tale Theatre* to see how the Disney model is slavishly copied or influences the work of contemporary filmmakers. This influence may be due in part to the production conditions of the film industry itself and the cultural values of the country. Whatever the case may be, the fairy-tale film must be viewed not only as a manifestation of the film institution but as part of the genre as institution. Today, this genre identification means that whereas a given fairy tale film will be packaged as a commodity, it will be consumed by a public that continues to tell fairy tales (and many other stories) orally in all types of situations; is exposed to classical fairy tales as books, cassettes, videotapes, commercials, cartoons, comics, radio plays, musicals, operas, ballets, and video games; reinterprets the fairy tales according to correct reading, ideological conditioning, and personal taste; and produces its own kinds of fairy tales, wishing for the transformation of these tales into reality.

A productive reception and critical interpretation of a fairy-tale film, one that might "decommodify" the film as commodity, demands, at the very least, a historical consciousness. Criticism must recapture art and moments of truth despite the manner in which culture is administered to negate history and to make the present banal. In fact, in order for the viewer to determine whether there is something new, meaningful, and utopian in the fairy-tale film, he or she must know the origins of the story. For children, such knowledge is difficult because the fairy tale insinuates itself into their lives as "natural history." It is as though the film has always been there; it is part of their history. This insinuation is exactly why a critical historicizing of the fairy-tale film and fairy tales in general is so important even if the fairy tale is a contemporary production such as Michael Ende's *Never Ending Story* or William Goldman's *The Princess Bride*. In the case of traditional fairy tales adapted for the screen, a rereading of the text both by children and adults can lead to an enriched appreciation both of the film and of the text. Moreover, the reader/viewer gains a greater sense of the development of the fairy-tale genre as an institution. In the case of Walt Disney's *Pinocchio*, this historical approach calls for a step back in history to explore Carlo Collodi's life and times, the conditions under which he produced his fairy-tale novel, the significance that it assumed in Italian culture, and the manner in which Disney "Americanized" *Pinocchio*.

If one were to believe Walt Disney's *American* film version of *Pinocchio* (1940), the wooden puppet turned human is a very happy boy in the end. After numerous adventures, Pinocchio learns that honesty is the best policy, a message repeatedly driven home by the film. Yet the 1882 *Italian* novel by Carlo Collodi is a much different affair. Pinocchio is indeed content to turn human at the end of the novel, but there is a tragicomic element to the episodes that make one wonder why the puppet must endure so much suffering to become a proper and honest boy. Did Collodi intend to make an example out of Pinocchio, the good-bad boy who must learn to assume responsibility for his actions? Or did he intend to show the harsh realities of peasant childhood in nineteenth-century Italy? Is Pinocchio perhaps a critical reflection of Collodi's own boyhood? After all, Carlo Collodi was not born to become a writer and journalist, nor was he born with the name Collodi. There was a fairy-tale element to his own education and development, and before we can fully understand why his Pinocchio, in contrast to Walt Disney's, is a tragicomic figure, we must examine Collodi's life and times.

Born Carlo Lorenzini in Florence on November 24, 1826, Collodi was raised in a lower-class family with nine brothers and sisters; only two of his siblings managed to survive childhood. His father and mother, Domenico and Angela Lorenzini, worked as servants for the Marquis Lorenzo Ginori, who paid for Collodi's education. In fact, without Ginori's help Collodi would never have gone to school. Collodi's parents were very poor and had so many children that Collodi, as the oldest, was sent to live with his grandparents in the little town of Collodi, outside Florence, where his mother had been born. When Collodi was ten, Ginori offered financial aid to send the boy to the seminary at Colle Val d'Elsa to study for the priesthood, but Collodi discovered that he was not cut out to be a priest, given his mischievous nature and dislike of monastic discipline. So, by the time he was sixteen, Collodi began studying philosophy and rhetoric at the College of the Scolopi Fathers in Florence and two years later found a position at the Libreria Piatti, a leading bookstore, where he helped prepare catalogues for Giuseppe Aiazzi, one of Italy's leading manuscript specialists. During this time Collodi met intellectuals and literary critics and developed an interest in literature. In 1848, however, he was carried away by revolutionary zeal to fight for Italian independence against the Austrians. After the defeat of the Italian forces that same year, he was fortunate enough to obtain a position as a civil servant in the municipal government while also working as a journalist, editor, and dramatist. In 1853 he founded the satirical political magazine *Il Lampione* (*The Street Lamp*), intended to enlighten the Italians about political oppression, but this publication was soon banned because his polemical writings were considered subversive by the Grand Duchy, which was loyal to the Austrian authorities. Not easily defeated, Collodi started a second journal, *Lo Scaramuccia* (*The Controversy*, 1854), which dealt more with theater and the arts than politics and lasted until 1858. Aside from publishing numerous articles, he also tried his hand at writing comedies but did not have much success. Indeed, he was more successful at politics and became known as an activist in liberal circles.

When the Second War of Independence erupted in 1859, Collodi volunteered for the cavalry, and this time the Italians were victorious. Not only were the Austrians defeated in northern Italy but the entire country was united under Giuseppe Garibaldi in 1861. During the period 1859–1861 Collodi, still known primarily as Lorenzini, became involved in a dispute about the new Italian unification with Professor Eugenio Alberi of Pisa, a reputable political writer, and he signed his defense of a unified Italy, a booklet titled *Il signor Alberi ha ragione! Dialogo apologetico* (1860), with the pseudonym *Collodi* in honor of his mother's native village, where he had spent his childhood. It was the first time he used this name, not realizing that it would become world-famous mainly through the later publication of a children's book.

Though convinced that unification was a positive step for Italy, Collodi soon discovered that the social changes he had expected for all Italians were not about to take place. Instead, the nobility profited most from the defeat of the Austrians, and corruption continued in the government, which supported the development of industry and the wealthy classes. He himself was fortunate because he was able to keep his position as a civil servant from 1860 to 1881 in the Commission of Theatrical Censorship and in the Prefecture of Florence. These appointments enabled him to serve as the stage director of the Teatro della Pergola in Florence and on the editorial committee that began research for an encyclopedia of Florentine dialect. However, Collodi, who still wrote mainly under the name of Lorenzini, did not give up his career as a journalist and freelance writer. In fact, he published several stories in *Io Fanfulla, Almanacco per il 1876* and in *Il Novelliere* (both 1876), which were reworked into sardonic sketches of Florentine life in *Macchiette* (*Sketches*, 1879), the first book he published under the pseudonym Collodi. In addition, he translated eighteenth-century French fairy tales by Charles Perrault, Mme. D'Aulnoy, and Mme. Le Prince de Beaumont under the title *I raconti delle fate* in 1876 and began reworking the didactic tales of the eighteenth-century Italian writer Parravinci in his book *Giannettino* (*Little Johnnie*) in 1879, which led to a series: *Il viaggio per l'Italia* (*Little Johnnie's Travels Through Italy*, 1880), *La Grammatica di Giannettino* (*Little Johnnie's Grammar Book*, 1882), *L'abbaco di Giannettino* (*Little Johnnie's Arithmetic Book*, 1885), *La geografia di Giannettino* (*Little Johnnie's Geog-*

raphy, 1886), and others, all published as textbooks for elementary schoolchildren.

Collodi's fairy-tale translations and textbooks prepared the way for his writing of *Pinocchio*, which was not initially conceived as a book. Collodi was asked in the summer of 1881 by the editors of a weekly magazine for children, *Il giornale per i bambini* (*Newspaper for Children*), to write a series of stories, and he began the first installment in July of that year under the title *Storia di un burattino* (*Story of a Puppet*). During the next two years Collodi continued to submit stories about Pinocchio to the magazine, and in 1883 they were gathered together in book form and published by Felice Paggi as *The Adventures of Pinocchio*. Though the book was an immense success and had gone through four editions by the time Collodi died in 1890, Collodi himself did not profit much from the publication because of the lack of good copyright laws to protect authors.

The book was first translated into English in 1892 by Mary Alice Murray, and by the mid-twentieth century it had been printed in a hundred different languages, abridged, bowdlerized, parodied, and adapted for stage, film, and television.[6] Such widespread popularity may be due to the fact that *Pinocchio* appears to be a symbolic narrative of boyhood that transcends its Italian origin and speaks to young and old about the successful rise of a ne'er-do-well. It is the consummate Horatio Alger story of the nineteenth century, a pull-yourself-up-by-your-own-bootstraps fairy tale that demonstrates that even a log has the potential to be good, human, and socially useful. Yet it is also a story of punishment and conformity, a tale in which a puppet without strings has strings of social constraint attached so that he will not go his own way but will respond to the pulls of superior forces, symbolized by the Blue Fairy and Geppetto. It is from the tension of the tragicomic that Pinocchio as a character lives and appeals to all audiences. Most important, it is the fairy-tale structure, which provides the episodes with their form and optimistic veneer, that makes us forget how grueling and traumatic boyhood can be, especially boyhood in late-nineteenth-century Italy.

It is important to remember the unique manner in which Collodi began *Pinocchio*:

Once upon a time there was ...

"A king!" my young readers will say right away.

No, children, that's where you're wrong. Once upon a time there was a piece of wood![7]

This beginning indicated that Collodi, like William Thackeray (*The Rose and the Ring*, 1855), Lewis Carroll (*Alice's Adventures in Wonderland*, 1865), and George MacDonald (*The Princess and the Goblin*, 1872), who had been experimenting in England, was about to expand upon the fairy-tale tradition in a most innovative manner. Collodi fused genres based on the oral folk tale and the literary fairy tale to create his own magical land inhabited by bizarre creatures. By turning genres and the real world upside down, he sought to question the social norms of his times and to interrogate the notion of boyhood.

In his use of folklore, Collodi consciously played with the tradition of "Jack tales," which generally deal with a naive, well-intentioned lad who, despite the fact that he is not too bright, manages to lead a charmed life and survives all sorts of dangerous encounters. Sometimes he becomes rich and successful at the end of the story. For the most part he is content just to return home safe and sound. In Italy there are numerous oral tales about bungling peasants whose naïveté is a blessing and paradoxically enables them to overcome difficulties in adventure after adventure. In Tuscany, the region where Collodi grew up, there were many tales about Florentines such as the one told by Italo Calvino in *Italian Folktales* in which a young Florentine feels like a blockhead because he has never been away from Florence and has no adventures to recount. After he leaves and travels about, however, he is almost murdered when he encounters a ruthless giant. Fortunately he escapes, but he loses a finger in the process. When he returns to Florence, he is cured of his urge to travel. What is significant in all the "Jack tales," no matter what their country or region of origin, is that the essential "goodness" of the protagonist—his good nature—protects him from evil forces, and in many cases, he learns to use his wits to trick the enemies who want to deceive or exploit him.

In the literary fairy-tale tradition of Europe, "Jack tales" are not prevalent because literary fairy tales were generally written first for upper-class audiences and mainly for adults, and bungling peasant heroes were not of particular interest to the educated classes. However, noses were, and Collodi knew about the noses from French fairy tales, some of which he had translated. For instance, in Charles Perrault's "The Foolish Wishes," a woodcutter's wife is cursed when her husband makes a bad wish and a sausage is attached to her nose. In Mme. Le Prince de Beaumont's "Prince Désir," a prince is born with a very long nose and compels everyone in his kingdom to think that long noses are the best in the world until an old fairy punishes him for his arrogance and vanity. The motif of the unusual nose was obviously appealing to Collodi, but it was not the nose alone that made *Pinocchio* so unique. Rather it is his combination of the folklore and literary fairy-tale traditions to reflect upon the situation of illiterate, playful, *poor* boys during the latter half of the nineteenth century in Italy that makes his narrative so compelling. Moreover, Collodi never wrote simply for an audience of young readers. His work was intended to appeal to children and adults and to suggest a mode of educating young boys, especially when they did not seem fit to be educated.

Read as a type of bildungsroman, or fairy-tale novel of development, *Pinocchio* can be interpreted positively as a representation of how peasant boys, when given a chance, can assume responsibility for themselves and their families and become industrious members of society. After all, Pinocchio is literally carved out of wood—out of an inanimate substance—and turns miraculously into a human boy who becomes responsible for the welfare of his poor father. This theme of education or development, however, is complex, for Collodi had not initially planned to allow Pinocchio to develop. In fact, he intended to end the series printed in *Il giornale per i bambini* at chapter 15 in which Pinocchio is left hanging on an oak tree, ostensibly dead. Yet, when this episode appeared in the November 10, 1881, issue of the newspaper with "finale" printed at the end, there was such a storm of protest from readers young and old that Collodi was forced to resume Pinocchio's adventures in the February 16, 1882, issue of the newspaper. In other words, Collodi was forced to "develop" or "educate" his wooden protagonist despite his initial pessimistic perspective. Therefore, though the development of a piece of wood into a young boy is the central theme of *Pinocchio*, it is a theme that the author ironically questioned from the very beginning of the protagonist's adventures, just as he questioned the optimistic structure of the fairy tale. This questioning accounts for the tension between skepticism and optimism in the novel. Moreover, the very structure of the episodes also contributes to the tension because they were never intended to culminate in a novel, just as Pinocchio was never intended to become human.

Collodi conceived each chapter for the newspaper so as to keep his readers interested in the strange fate of a "live" piece of wood that is turned into a puppet. He maintained this interest with irony and suspense. Though the specific events are not predictable, all the episodes have the same plan: Each begins with a strange situation that leads to a near tragedy and borders on the ridiculous. However, in Collodi's topsy-turvy fairy-tale world, which faintly resembled Tuscany but constantly changed shape, anything is possible. Moreover, Collodi mischievously plays with the readers by leaving them hanging in suspense at the end of each chapter. In fact, each episode is a predicament, and one predicament leads to the next. No chapter is ever finished, and even the end of the book can be considered unfinished, for it is uncertain what lies ahead of Pinocchio after he turns human. He is still a boy. He has very little money. He is not educated. There is no indication that he will prosper as in a traditional fairy tale, even though he has developed a sense of responsibility and compassion. Pinocchio has survived boyhood and has been civilized to take the next step into manhood—but it is uncertain where this step may lead.

Given the unfinished business of Pinocchio's development, Collodi's major and constant question throughout this fairy-tale novel of education is whether it is indeed worthwhile to become "civilized." It is a question that Mark Twain was asking about the same time when he wrote *The Adventures of Huckleberry Finn*, and in some ways Huck Finn is the American version of Pinocchio, for both boys are brutally exposed to the hypocrisy of society and yet compelled to adapt to the values and standards that will allegedly enable them to succeed. Huck refuses civilization in the end, while Pinocchio appears to make peace with law and order.

Ultimately, Collodi asks us to consider how such socialization occurs, and if we examine how the "innocent" piece of wood, whose vices consist of playfulness and naïveté, is treated by the people and social forces around him, then there is something almost tragic in the way he is beaten and lulled into submission. From the beginning, Pinocchio's destiny is stamped by the fact that Geppetto carves him into a boy puppet because he wants to make money using the puppet as his meal ticket. Simply put, his father "gives birth" to Pinocchio because he wants to earn a living through him. Geppetto has no interest in learning who his son is and what his desires are. His son is an investment in his own future. Geppetto is not an uncaring father, but his relationship to Pinocchio is ambivalent because of his initial "desire" to create a puppet that will know how to dance, fence, and turn somersaults so that he can earn a crust of bread and a glass of wine. In other words, Pinocchio is supposed to please his creator, and Geppetto literally holds the strings to the puppet's fate in his hands. In chapter 7, after Pinocchio has lost his feet, Geppetto at first refuses to make new feet for him until Pinocchio says, "I promise you, father, that I'll learn a trade and be the comfort and staff of your old age."[8] Geppetto complies with Pinocchio's wish, and the puppet shows his gratitude by expressing his desire to go to school. He is extremely moved when Geppetto then sells his own coat to purchase a spelling book required for school. Collodi comments, "And although Pinocchio was a very good-humored boy, even he became sad, because poverty, when it is true poverty, is understood by everyone—even by children."[9]

On the one hand, Pinocchio wants to be—and is—socialized to please his father; on the other hand, he cannot control his natural instincts to explore the world and to seek pleasure. Caught in a predicament—to please his father means to deny his own pleasures—Pinocchio as a *poor, illiterate peasant boy* must learn the "ups and downs of the world," as Geppetto puts it; that is, he must be physically subdued and put in his place until he functions properly as an industrious worker, his rebellious instincts curbed. Collodi clearly demonstrates in a very specific class analysis that poor Italian boys of this period had very little choice if they wanted to advance in life. Using Pinocchio as a symbolic figure, Collodi torments and punishes the puppet each time Pinocchio veers from the norm of acceptable behavior. Among his punishments are the loss of his legs through burning; the expansion of his nose as a consequence of lying; being hung from an oak tree; imprisonment for four months; being caught in a trap and used by a farmer as a watchdog; being caught in a net and almost fried as a fish by the Green Fisherman; being transformed into a donkey; being compelled to work in a circus; being drowned to escape skinning; and being swallowed by a gigantic shark.

These forms of punishment in the novel are, of course, so preposterous that readers can take delight in and laugh at the events. At the same time, the laughter is mixed with relief that the readers do not have to undergo such tortures themselves. Besides, the laughter is instructive, for readers learn what to avoid through Pinocchio's mistakes, and they learn how to attain dignity. It is this attainment of self-dignity as a human being that is most crucial at the end of Pinocchio's adventures. As in most fairy-tale narratives, Pinocchio is obliged to fulfill specific tasks to gain his reward, and two are primary: First, Pinocchio must rescue his father, Geppetto; and second, he must keep his promises to the Blue Fairy by showing that he can be obedient, honest, and industrious. Despite his suffering, he perseveres and earns the recognition of the Blue Fairy. He also learns to distinguish between good and bad, between ridiculous puppet and responsible boy behavior. In this regard, Collodi's narrative is a fairy-tale novel of development that makes a sober statement despite its humor and grotesque scenes.

For readers of Collodi's time, who were largely from the middle and educated classes, *Pinocchio* represented a warning to mischievous scamps and set a model of proper behavior. Collodi himself may have viewed *Pinocchio* in part as representing the difficulties he himself had experienced and had had to overcome in order to be accepted in Florentine society of his time, a perspective that other readers from the lower classes may have shared. For today's readers, Collodi's *Pinocchio* may come as a surprise, for most are probably shocked to find that the novel is not the same as the Disney film, which they have probably seen before reading Collodi's original work. They will realize that Collodi let his imagination run wild more than Disney did and that he developed his puppet in more extraordinary ways. Indeed, thanks to Collodi's wild imagination, we have a rich commentary on what it meant to develop as a peasant boy in nineteenth-century Italian society. But more important, perhaps, his fairy-tale novel transcends history and continues to raise questions about how we "civilize" children in uncivilized times.

Here we turn to the "tamed" imagination of Disney, who also pondered the question of civilizing children in barbaric times. His youth was spent, in part, contending with a self-righteous, exploitative father and deferential mother; serving in the army during World War I while being abandoned by his sweetheart; and trying to establish himself as a leading film animator in the 1920s with very little money and in cutthroat competition with other filmmakers, distributors, and producers.[10] Though there is certainly a rebellious and adventurous side to his silent films of the 1920s—his fairy-tale films of 1922–1923 are witty, unique, and explosive[11]—he took a more conservative approach to fairy tales in the 1930s with the apparent intention of capturing larger audiences. Since he wanted to impress the public with his artistic techniques and technological inventions, he had to find stories that were widely acceptable to audiences, not only in America but throughout the world. Given the fact that these were the Depression years, filled with social strife and misery, when fascism had already reared its ugly head throughout the world, Disney's choice of content for his films indicated that he wanted to offer hope in the form of beautifully made films that provided escape from the grim realities of America at that time, or reconciliation with these realities. To a certain extent, he ignored what was happening to the majority of families in the United States and provided models of social adaptation. Obsessed with his own art and with developing his company, Disney succeeded in gathering around him some of the finest artists, animators, musicians, technicians, and writers in the business to produce *Snow White and the Seven Dwarfs* in 1937 and *Pinocchio* in 1940, the two major projects that occupied him throughout the 1930s.

It is important, of course, to bear in mind that a Disney film was his in name only. That is, Disney's authorship was not total. In the case of *Pinocchio*, the idea for the making of the film came early in 1937 from Norm Ferguson, a member of the studio staff, and Disney became enthusiastic about the project after he read Collodi's fairy-tale novel. His main concern, however, was to find a way to utilize the newly developed multiplane camera and to introduce innovative techniques in animation.[12] Work began on the production in 1937 but was stopped for a brief period because Disney was not satisfied with the animators' early results. The original Collodi story line was proving to be too complex to streamline, and Richard Wunderlich and Thomas Morrissey have argued that it was not until Disney saw Yasha Frank's musical *Pinocchio: A Musical Legend* in June of 1937 that he embraced the idea of the film wholeheartedly: "Disney consciously created a story line different from Frank's but took the new image of Pinocchio and Geppetto from Frank. Disney's decision was deliberate and well thought out. Furthermore, Disney was clearly conscientious in his endeavor to know Collodi's tale. Not only did he acquire the Italian original and various editions and adaptations of the translations, but—perhaps to be sure of the material—he also contracted for his own translation."[13]

A key for Disney in reshaping Frank's musical and the Collodi material was to make the relationship between father and son more harmonious and tender; to "Americanize" the representation of boyhood itself; and to simplify the plot so that his moral code of success based on conforming to the dictates of good behavior and diligence could be transmitted through song, dance, and rounded images of tranquility. Richard Schickel remarks that

> one must suspect that Disney found in this story elements of autobiography, since he had himself been a child denied the normal prerogatives of boyhood. It is certainly possible that at least some portion of his drive for success was a compensation for his failure to find the father who had, in the psychological sense, been lost to him since childhood.... Such an interpretation suggests why *Pinocchio* is the darkest in hue of all Disney's pictures and the one which, despite its humor, is the most consistently terrifying. The menacing

whips that crack over the heads of the boys who are turned into donkeys after their taste of the sybaritic life may have their origin in his recurrent nightmare of punishment for failure to deliver his newspapers. And, of course, one suspects the dream of winning the neglectful father's approval by a heroic act—such as rescuing him from a living death in the whale's maw—must have occurred to Disney at some point in his unhappy youth.[14]

It is obviously somewhat misleading (and yet compelling) to identify Disney with Pinocchio and his father with Geppetto, for we know that numerous hands played a role in designing the characters and story line of the film under Disney's supervision.[15] But this is all the more reason to focus on the image of the boy Pinocchio and how he is socialized to represent "the American boy" because if Disney and his staff worked together on projecting what it takes to be a good boy—or what Douglas Street insightfully calls a pipsqueak in contrast to Collodi's picaro[16]—then this figure represents the product of a particular group of American male artists reflecting on what it means to be a good boy and a good son in their society. To this extent, the father-son relationship and boyhood as depicted in the pictures, edited, and projected on the screen represent more than just Disney's wish-fulfillments and desires. As model characters Geppetto and Pinocchio are idealistic projections, corrections to the reality of boyhood in America, but one wonders whether such correct relations and behavior in the Disney remake of Collodi's work are as exemplary as they seem. After all, they suggest the benefits of conformity and the nullification of individual experimentation with reality to gain a sense of one's particular drives and identity vis-à-vis social demands.

In his streamlined reduction of the Collodi novel, Disney shifted the role of the cricket, ignominiously killed by Pinocchio in the Italian version, to that of moral conscience. In fact, Jiminy Cricket is the major character in Disney's film. He frames and narrates the story; his voice becomes the authentic fairy-tale voice. His dictates as moral conscience are imposed on Pinocchio and the audience at the same time. He is like the sympathetic vaudeville clown, charming and naive, who wins the audience over through his comic routines that always have him stumbling but landing on his feet. From the beginning we know that he will triumph because he has already survived his adventures with Pinocchio and lives to tell that wishes can come true. His omniscient narrative voice is a soothing, didactic one that explains what one must do to transform oneself from an inexperienced, foolish puppet to a good little human boy. The difficulty with his story is that Pinocchio the puppet is uninteresting, if not boring, and that Jiminy Cricket must provide the spark and excitement in the story.

This story was superbly condensed by Disney and his collaborators. If we study its structure based on a triad of adventures—three is the fairy-tale lucky number—we can see that the tale is carefully constructed to follow the classical form. After the hero's initial birth, he is obliged to depart, ostensibly to go to school, but in reality this departure marks the beginning of three adventures of conflict and escape: (1) Pinocchio's servitude in the marionette theater and escape from Stromboli; (2) the trip to Pleasure Island, where Pinocchio is semitransformed into a donkey and the escape via sea to the mainland; (3) the search for Pinocchio's father and escape from the whale. At the end, Pinocchio is rewarded for his unselfish act (saving his father at sea) by rising from the dead and becoming a real boy. Pinocchio is safe at home, and his conscience, Jiminy Cricket, is rewarded for work well done.

This straightforward, simple story line is enhanced by the extraordinary camera work that relied on the multiplane camera to zoom in and out and provide depth in all the key scenes of the village, theater, Pleasure Island, the whale, and the sea. The songs and dance scenes reinforce the didactic lessons in an amusing manner, while the minor characters such as Figaro the cat and Cleo the goldfish add a light touch to the action that often borders on the tragic. Here, of course, Stromboli, the rogues Honest John and Kitty, the Lord of Pleasure Island, and Monstro are remarkable creations of villainy who symbolically represent the "evil father." If Schickel is correct in assuming that there are autobiographical undertones in this film, then more must be made out of the evil father, who indeed may have been closer to Disney's real father than Geppetto. Taken together as aspects of the "bad father," the sinister figures represent dishonesty, exploitation for profit, and greed, whereas Geppetto is sincerity, nurturing love, and sacrifice. One could even argue that there is something "motherly" or feminine about him. But truly, in this all-male cast of characters—the fairy and the fish remain in the background—Pinocchio must learn to choose which male models to follow and which to disregard. He comes into the social world like Casper Hauser or the Wolf Child, an innocent, a natural creature who must learn how to speak and to identify words with things and actions with moral implications. Without a conscience to guide him, he would be lost.

It is the voice of conscience that makes the Disney film so fascinating and complex. Few critics have paid attention to the fact that while Jiminy Cricket is the narrator of the story, it is the fairy who holds power and intervenes to reward and punish according to the code of bravery, truth, and unselfishness. She is the supreme nurturer and judge who literally pulls all the strings to safeguard Pinocchio's future. She intervenes to settle the strife among sons and fathers, or at the very least to point Pinocchio in the right direction so he can succeed in his endeavor to become a "real boy."

The maternal, soothing voice of the fairy is reinforced by the gentle voice of the cricket, who is not only a friend but also a father figure. In fact, the organized forces of fairy/cricket/clockmaker and their voices merge and form the model parent for Pinocchio, who is reborn at the end of the film to reenter the world as a finished product that will not make any mistakes. Pinocchio is the perfect, charming good boy when he awakens in his bed, but he is almost too perfect to be true. Like a doll that has been mass produced and is ready to be taken home from the shelf of a store, he is the dream toy that Geppetto has wished for, prefabricated by the fairy's instructions and endowed with a moral conscience also supplied by the fairy.

This is the irony at the end of Disney's *Pinocchio*: The unreal puppet who was believable becomes a boy who is too real to be true. Disney and his collaborators produce before our eyes the making of a perfect "American" boy. Though the film appears to take place in Tyrol—the father speaks with a German accent and the village and scenery are reminiscent of Tyrol and northern Italy—

the voice and mannerisms of Pinocchio are clearly more American than European. It is almost as if the Old World is giving birth to something newer and more honest than decadent Europe. But what is new in *Pinocchio* is really old, for Disney's boy is carved out to be obedient, diligent, and honest, not "bad" virtues in themselves, but in the context of the story these virtues take on a masochistic character. Like many "gifted" children, Pinocchio will aim to please and will repress his desires and wishes to ensure first and foremost that his father is happy. Such a boy is easily manipulated for the good of the country, the good of the corporation, and the good of the Disney studio.

In the course of the development of the fairy-tale film during the twentieth century, *Pinocchio* is pivotal because the content of the film and the film as product reveal major changes in the institutionalization of the fairy tale as genre. What was important for Disney was *not* the immediate and personal contact of a storyteller with a particular audience to share wisdom and induce pleasure but the impact that he as creator could have on as large an audience as possible in order to sell a commodity and endorse ideological images that would enhance his corporate power. The fairy tale became an advertisement for a trademark, and this trademark denoted what the virtues of family fare should be and how amusement was to be structured. The fairy-tale film capitalizes on a vast variety of transformations in related fields of theater, radio, opera, ballet, and music and is certainly not always as one-dimensionally structured as most of the Disney fairy-tale films are. But the tendency to make a commodified spectacle out of the oral and literary tradition predominates. Disney was only one among many filmmakers who saw fairy tales as a source of money, just as many parents see their children as an investment in their own future. The connection between abusive parents in fairy tales and abusive filmmakers who use fairy tales about abusive parents to absolve themselves from the responsibility of taking fairy tales seriously is rarely made, but it is a connection that might help us make distinctions between fairy-tale films as commodities and as art in our present-day struggles to determine what is politically and culturally "correct" for children.

4

Once Upon a Time
beyond Disney

Contemporary Fairy-Tale Films
for Children

Without question, Walt Disney set the standards for feature-length fairy-tale films in the world of cinema. After his beginnings during the 1920s in Kansas City, where he and Ub Iwerks made several shorts such as *Puss in Boots*, *Cinderella*, *Little Red Riding Hood*, and *The Bremen Town Musicians*, Disney moved to Hollywood and began perfecting the techniques of animation, organizing his studio along the lines of efficient modern factories, and experimenting with story lines that would appeal to large audiences of all age groups and social classes. By 1934 he was finally ready to produce the film that would institutionalize the fairy-tale genre in the cinema industry in a manner that was just as revolutionary as the collecting and editing of the Brothers Grimm had been for the print industry in the nineteenth century: *Snow White and the Seven Dwarfs* (1937) was the first animated feature in history based on a fairy tale and made in color with music. Moreover, as a mass-market commodity with the trademark "Disney," it was created with such technological and artistic skill that the Disney Studios have been able to retain a market stranglehold on fairy-tale films up to the present. Any other filmmaker who has endeavored to adapt a fairy tale for the screen, whether through animation or other means, has had to measure up to the Disney standard and try to go beyond it.

But just what is the Disney standard, or, rather, the Disney standardized fairy tale? Since all Disney fairy-tale films are alike, from *Snow White* of 1937 to *The Lion King* of 1994, it may be more appropriate to talk about standardization than about standards.

In fact, the success of the Disney fairy tale from 1937 to the present is attributable not to Disney's uncanny ability to retell nineteenth-century fairy tales with originality and uniqueness but to his intuitive genius, which made use of the latest technological developments in the cinema to celebrate mechanical reproduction in animation and to glorify a particular American perspective on individualism and male prowess. In short, Disney "Taylorized" the extraordinary talents organized in his studios to represent himself as the prototypical American hero who cleans up the world in the name of goodness and justice. Embodied as the stalwart prince in all his fairy-tale films, Disney himself became the trademark and the product of technical animation controlled by corporate powers that communicated a single message: "What is good in the name of Disney is good for the rest of the world."

Not all Disney fairy-tale films are univocal and one-dimensional. As Eric Smoodin has convincingly argued in his important book *Animating Culture*, "Animation was not produced within a system of fixed institutions and social practices, practices which, as conventional wisdom might have it, always and unproblematically reduced cartoons to children's entertainment, or which uniformly enforced censorship restrictions. Instead, the Hollywood cartoon from the classical era developed from, expressed, and was frequently controlled by a number of shifting and often contradictory discourses, about, for instance, sexuality, race, gender, class, leisure and creativity."[1] Although Smoodin's study is concerned primarily with the short cartoon and how it was frequently placed in movie programs and changed through censorship for purposes of social control, his remarks are applicable to the animated fairy-tale feature film, and certainly he is correct in arguing that the meanings of each film could not be totally controlled by Disney or the Hollywood industry. Nevertheless, it is within the framework of power relations and the development of the culture industry that the reception, interpretation, and discussions of the films take place. That is, the filmmakers' creative intentions are governed by a structural network of production for profit to which they appeal and against which they rebel, and this network is built into the very plots and narratives of the fairy-tale films.

Most important for Disney and other producers of fairy-tale films was the manner in which they could "hook" children as consumers not because they believed their films had artistic merit and could contribute to children's cultural development, but because they wanted to control children's aesthetic interests and consumer tastes. Richard deCordova makes this point quite clear in his essay "The Mickey in Macy's Window: Childhood, Consumerism, and Disney Animation": "From the late 1920s to the middle 1930s there was an intensification and rationalization of the process through which films were linked to consumer goods. Such organizations as Hollywood Associates and the Modern Merchandising Bureau emerged to coordinate the display of fashions in Hollywood films and fan magazines with the subsequent production and marketing of those fashions to the public. And the studio exploitation departments systematically began to conceive of story ideas and scripts as opportunities for a wide range of lucrative product tie-ins."[2]

DeCordova points out that in the early 1930s the child was regarded as a consumer in a double sense—consumer of films and consumer of products displayed through films. All studios with children as target audiences developed elaborate networks of mutual reference between these two levels of consumption so that it has become common practice today to market most fairy-tale films for children with books, cassettes, t-shirts, ties, jewelry, porcelain figures, plates, toothbrushes, school supplies, toys, underwear, pajamas, and even books. Such marketing has become so common that we rarely think twice about it, though there were major debates in the 1930s about the effect such films and practices had on children. And it was in the 1930s that the Mickey Mouse Clubs were formed to contribute to such consumerism.

By 1937 everything was in place for Disney to tirelessly convey and reinforce his trademark message in all the animated fairy-tale films and other cinematic products of his studios. In fact, as early as 1934 the American magazine *Fortune* was able to state with remarkable perspicacity, "In Disney's studio a twentieth-century miracle is achieved: by a system as truly of the machine age as Henry Ford's plant at Dearborn, true art is produced. Hereafter we shall examine that system and see how it resembles and how it differs from the automatic simplicity of an assembly line."[3] Though the *Fortune* article maintained that the final products of the Disney studio were artfully manufactured, it also demonstrated that the films were made not for the sake of exploring the story as an art form or for the sake of educating children and stimulating their imaginations but for the sake of promoting the Disney label. There was very little difference in emphasis then, as now, between a Disney plate, watch, t-shirt, cap, or amusement park filled with other commodities and rides and the fairy tales that he adapted for film and book publication. The copyrighted label was what counted most. Disney's signature designating ownership of the fairy-tale films was part of his "modern" endeavor to re-create an ancient mythic cult through mechanical reproduction. What is perhaps most striking about Disney's fairy-tale films, unlike his other inventions and commodities, is that he avowedly sought to make the characters and background as lifelike as possible, and the more he attempted to do so, the more his versions of the classical fairy tales became lifeless.

Indeed, Disney's re-creation of himself had a result opposite to fairy tales' traditional message, for they illustrate how people and things can be magically restored to life, whereas he transformed himself from a living being into a brand name that became synonymous with what Nietzsche called "the eternal return of the *same*," in Disney's case the eternal return of the same kind of youth. There is something peculiarly American about this striving to remain forever young and blissful in Disney's fairy-tale films that perhaps accounts for their appeal. However, the films continually package youth and bliss in the same manner so that the end effect is homogeneity in perfect synchronization.

All of the Disney Studios fairy-tale films focus on synchronization, one-dimensionality, and uniformity for the purpose of maintaining the Disney brand name as champion of entertainment. If we were to study each one of the studio's fairy-tale films from *Snow White* to *The Lion King*, we would discover the following similar features:

1. Each film is a musical that imitates the standard Hollywood musical of the 1930s. Special attention is paid to catchy lyrics and tunes, background music, and sound effects that either heighten or break the action so that the characters can reveal their innermost thoughts. For instance, Snow White sings about wishing for a prince, and Beauty announces that she wants to break out of her provincial town and find the love of her life. As Richard Schickel has remarked,

   > There is also a structural rigidity about the Disney animated features that has grown increasingly obvious as the years have passed. The editing principles applied to *Snow White* were those of the conventionally well-made commercial film of the time. There was nothing particularly daring about the way it was put together; its merit was based on other skills. In general, a scene would open with an establishing or master shot, then proceed to an intermediate shot, then to close-ups of the various participants, with conventional cut-aways to various details of scenery or decor as needed. Confusing flashbacks or dream sequences were avoided, and special effects were introduced in such a way that every child was aware that something out of the ordinary was about to happen.[4]

2. The sequential arrangement of the frames, with clear breaks between each scene, follows the same prescribed plot: The disenfranchised or oppressed heroine *must* be rescued by a daring prince. Heterosexual happiness and marriage are always the ultimate goals of the story. There is no character development because all characters must be recognizable as types that remain unchanged throughout the film. Good cannot become evil, nor can evil become good. The world is viewed in Manichaean terms as a dichotomy, and only the good will inherit the earth.

3. Since the basic plot is always the same, the incidental characters and their antics play an important role in the film version of the story. They are always funny, adorable, infantile, and mischievous. They are the dwarfs and animals in *Snow White*; the mice and fairy godmother in *Cinderella*; the household utensils in *Beauty and the Beast*; the genie and animals in *Aladdin*. Their slapstick humor and marvelous feats place the technical wonders of the film on display and prevent the fairy tale from becoming boring. Since nothing new is told or explored in the story, there is always a danger that it will become boring.

4. What passes as new is the introduction of innovative camera work, improved color, greater synchronization, livelier music and lyrics, and unique drawings of exotic characters. Yet this "newness" reinforces the nostalgia for eternal youth and a well-ordered, clean world in which evil is always recognizable and good takes the form of a male hero who is as dependable as the phallic principles that originally stamped the medium of animation at the beginning of the twentieth century.[5]

5. Disney's films were never intended solely for children but were meant to captivate the "child" in all the viewers. If one can discern an attitude toward children in the films, it is that they are to be swept away as objects by the delightful and erotic images. This sweeping away is an envelopment that involves loss of identity; that is, children as viewers are to lose themselves in the oedipal wishes that are depicted on the screen. The process of viewing involves infantilization because each frame regulates the drives and wishes of the viewer according to rigid sexist and racist notions that emanate from the nineteenth century and are recalled in the film with nostalgia.

Since Disney never really wanted to explore the narrative depths of the fairy tale through cinema but instead wanted to celebrate the technics of animation itself and to figure prominently as the divine power behind these technics, he left an opening for other filmmakers who have sought to go beyond Disney in re-creating fairy tales for the screen, with varying success. They range from Jean Cocteau to Jim Henson and have used both realistic means and animation to focus more on changing the tale than reestablishing its antiquated view of the world. In light of the fact that there have been hundreds of fairy-tale films produced for both children and adults since 1937, it would be extremely difficult to discuss all the experiments that have sought to transcend the standardized Disney film. Therefore, I want to focus on some of the more recent endeavors of such filmmakers as Jim Henson, Shelley Duvall, and Tom Davenport, who have tried to produce "high-quality" fairy-tale films for young viewers. Indeed, these filmmakers, though marked by Disney, have different attitudes toward children as viewers, and instead of using the film medium to infantilize them, they have produced films that seek to challenge children and to make them think and act for themselves. Their success (or lack of it) cannot be measured by breaking the Disney stranglehold on the fairy-tale film because no studio can really challenge Disney Studios' corporate power over the means of distribution and the market for fairy-tale films. Even Henson Productions had to realize this fact after Jim Henson died in 1991.[6] However, other filmmakers' success can truly be measured by their artistic use of innovative narrative strategies to deviate from the "Disney standards."

Jim Henson

Until his sudden death in 1991, Jim Henson and his associates appeared to be the greatest challenge to the Disney Studios in developing animated and live-action shows for children that not only captured their pocketbooks but managed to stimulate their minds as well. More daring and innovative than the Disney films, the productions of Henson Associates covered a wide variety of topics and tapped the technical possibilities of puppetry, animation, and acting to challenge the creative and critical capabilities of young viewers, whether through *Sesame Street*, which was telecast on American public broadcasting service from 1969 to 1981; *The*

Muppet Show, which ran on American television from 1976 to 1981; the films *The Muppet Movie* (1979) and *The Great Muppet Caper* (1981); or the television production *The Storyteller* (1987).

Henson experimented with fairy tales in different ways by parodying the classical and Disney traditions through his Muppet characters and by addressing serious concerns of history, folklore, and narration in his brief series *The Storyteller*. I want to discuss three examples of his work to demonstrate how the Henson films subverted the standards of Disney fairy-tale films to break through the Disney techniques of infantilization, narrative strategies of closure, and the exaltation of homogeneity.

The Frog Prince, directed and produced by Henson,[7] was telecast by CBS on May 11, 1971, and was later made into a videotape for distribution in North America. It is notable for its irreverent attitude toward the Grimms' version of "The Frog King" and is a critical transformation of the classical beast/bridegroom narrative that basically celebrates male authority. The Muppet film is told tongue-in-cheek from Kermit the Frog's perspective, and with the exception of live actors as the prince and princess, all of the roles are played by bizarre puppets who remain puppets. That is, the story is fantasy with no pretensions of the characters becoming lifelike or acting like real people, even though a frog puppet is transformed into a human being in the end.

The new story as fantasy reads as follows: Kermit, sitting by a pond, recalls an incident in which he encountered a tiny frog, a stranger named Robin, who tells him and the other frogs at the pond that he is an enchanted prince, bewitched by an evil motley witch and her sidekick, a dumb ogre named Sweetums. None of the frogs, including Kermit, believes him as he sings, "They call me Robin the brave, and history will one day rave. I'm noble and brave ..." Because Robin's such a runt of a frog, they all think his story is just a fairy tale, but Kermit soon realizes that he is telling the truth when he sees that Robin cannot swim.

Now, the only way that Robin can become human again is to be kissed by a princess who lives in a nearby castle. However, Kermit tells him that there is little chance because Princess Milora has also been bewitched and can only speak backward. But when she comes

to the pond and accidentally loses her golden ball, Robin promises
to retrieve it if she will take him to the castle and befriend him.
Since he promises not to cause any trouble, she gladly agrees, and
Robin miraculously gets the ball. Once at the castle, where Kermit continues his narration, we learn that the princess was cursed
by her Aunt Tamanella, who is none other than the witch who
had changed Robin and who has tricked the stupid king into
believing that she is his long-lost sister. Tamanella's eyes are on
the king's throne, and she seeks to be crowned as queen in
Princess Milora's place. To prevent any attempt at interference,
she captures Robin and gives him to Sweetums the Ogre to eat.
However, Kermit helps Robin escape, and along with the other
frogs of the pond, they intercede at the coronation of Tamanella
and smash the ball on the handle of the witch's cane. She loses
her powers, is transformed into a bird, and flies off. The princess,
who immediately regains her ability to speak correctly, thanks her
friends for their help and gives Robin a kiss. Of course, he is transformed into a prince, and the spectators sing a song of joy to celebrate the coronation of the princess. At the end, we are returned
to the pond where Kermit sits on the edge of the well and tells the
viewers that he still sees the prince and princess a lot. They appear
on the scene with a baby, and Kermit adds that he feels proud to
have a baby named after him.

This cinematic spoof of the Grimms' fairy tale is filled with
humorous songs such as the lullaby song for the ogre: "Go to sleep,
you stupid brute. / Lay your ugly head on your wretched bed. /
Close your eyes and go to sleep." There are also tender songs, such
as the princess's lyrical ditty about loneliness. Instead of reinforcing
notions about male sovereignty, the story is about friendship, kindness, and the exposure of authoritarianism and tyranny. The king
is benevolent but stupid; the witch is mean and nasty. The ogre is
nothing but brute force. They are overcome through the friendship
of the frogs, prince, and princess, who learn to trust each other
through the course of the action. This friendship is contrasted with
superficial and exploitative relationships. For instance, there are
two wonderfully droll scenes in which the king reads proclamations
to his subjects, who, like a television audience, must be prompted

to laugh, cheer, or sigh. Henson's film mocks such artificial prompting through his artful use of the puppets, who keep reminding us that they are playing with plots and roles.

This sense of play is also kept alive in other Henson films. For instance, in the thirty-minute animated film *Snow White and the Seven Muppets* (1988), part of *The Muppet Babies* series, there is a clear playful reference to Disney's *Snow White* right at the beginning of the film. The Muppets, all depicted as children, return to their home after seeing the film *Snow White*. Their nanny leaves them in the playroom, and they begin talking about the film and wanting to be actors. Kermit suggests that they put on their own play, and he assumes the role of director while the other well-known Muppet figures (Fozzie, Rowlf, Animal, Scooter, Beaker, Gonzo, Rizzo, etc.) begin dividing the parts. Of course, Miss Piggy wants to play Snow White, but she is opposed by Scooter. A coin is tossed and Miss Piggy loses, and this "loss" sets the tone for the rest of the play. Miss Piggy cannot stand losing, and she is vindictive in and outside the play.

As director, Kermit has his hands full trying to use the found objects in the room for the sets and to gain the cooperation of the other Muppets. Once the stage is set, Piggy admires herself in a mirror and states, "I'm so cute. I can't stand it." The next frame is a black and white documentary scene of crowds cheering. Kermit reminds Piggy about the plot. So she asks the mirror, played by Fozzie, who is the cutest in the world, and Fozzie replies, "I've got something to tell you you're not going to dig. You're just an ordinary pig." Hearing this response, Miss Piggy explodes and chases Fozzie off the stage until Kermit restores order, but after he calls for a change of scene, Animal lowers the background set upside down.

The remainder of the play continues in this chaotic manner, with all of the Muppets falling in and out of their roles. Miss Piggy calls for exterminators to wipe out the pest Snow White, who escapes to a beauty parlor where the dwarfs work. They promise to change her looks so no one will recognize her. However, eventually Miss Piggy as the witch finds Scooter as Snow White and scares her to death with a snake because she has run out of apples. The final scene depicts Scooter on a table with the dwarfs singing the "Snow

White Blues" and scraggly animals sobbing with the dwarfs in an obvious caricature of Disney's final scene. Kermit arrives on a black, mangy horse, which the others find inappropriate, but he responds by saying, "Don't blame me, blame Animal. He drew it." Since Kermit is now in the play, Miss Piggy chooses to become the director and won't let Kermit kiss Scooter. She changes the ending of the play twice by having the wolf from "Little Red Riding Hood" and the giant from "Jack and the Beanstalk" interfere. As the Muppet "actors" complain, the nanny enters the room, and after discovering that the Muppet children were rehearsing the play *Snow White*, she remarks that she has always wanted to play the witch. Miss Piggy is redeemed by this remark, and as the Muppets prepare to put on the play again, they all want to play the witch.[8]

The animation by Takashi in this Henson production is not highly inventive, but the explosive use of unexpected montage, the transformation of crude childlike drawings into workable sets, and the clever script by Jeffrey Scott all make for an extraordinary film about child's play and the creative manner in which children resolve their disputes through play. The classical *Snow White* is about a jealous conflict between an older woman and her young "rival" that only a prince can resolve, and the Henson film makes this conflict much more comprehensible for children by depicting the vain Miss Piggy as a sore loser who acts out jealousy in an imaginative play. Nor can Kermit as director or prince save Scooter/Snow White or bring about a resolution to the jealousy felt by Miss Piggy. There is no closure to this narrative, which is a rehearsal and will keep changing as the children are encouraged to explore the tale's manifold meanings.

Such creative exploration of narration has continually marked Henson's films. In his most unique contribution to the development of the fairy-tale film, *The Storyteller*, he took nine tales, mainly from the Grimms' collection, and produced them with the assistance of Anthony Minghella, who was responsible for the screenplays.[9] In an interview published in *American Film*, Henson remarked, "The stories we were telling were traditional folktales, and they could never be depicted literally because there's a lot of traveling and meeting giants and going to far countries. So we had to do a lot of storytelling through different shortcuts. There were a lot of interesting visual ways of telling the story. We did certain portions in silhouette, and other times we would just have the storyteller (played by John Hurt) *tell* the story instead of literally showing it."[10] The frame for all of these fairy-tale films is ingenious: The storyteller, a wizened, gray-haired man, sits by a fireplace and tells tales to a puppet dog, who skeptically poses questions and even intervenes during the storytelling. The dog as listener keeps the storyteller honest and on his toes, and when the story is finished, the dog expresses disbelief about the authenticity of the teller's sources. There is no absolute truth in these tales, yet there are truths built on contradictions and suggestive images that make the tales into compelling narratives worth viewing and reviewing: The Henson studios created tiny masterpieces that have set remarkable artistic standards for fairy-tale films by contravening traditional tales and Disney prescriptions.

Despite the fact that the frame for all of *The Storyteller* films is similar, the creative development of each tale is visually and technically so different that each film demands a long, detailed discussion. I shall therefore deal with just one of the films, "Hans My Hedgehog," to demonstrate how unique the Henson productions are.

The most popular version of "Hans My Hedgehog" is to be found in the Grimms' collection, and it is based on the beast/bridegroom type of folktale in which a young woman is obliged to sacrifice herself because her father has made a promise to a monster. The most well-known tale of this kind is "Beauty and the Beast," and the plot generally makes an equation of beauty = passivity = femininity, whereas ugliness is due to some curse and the victim is in need of salvation. The heroine is supposed to sacrifice herself for the welfare of her father or parents, and she is generally rewarded for being docile, virtuous, and obedient. In the Henson and Minghella cinematic version, various themes are explored in depth instead of the necessity for feminine sacrifice. With regard to the "monster," there is the hedgehog's personal struggle to overcome his bestial shape and form his own whole identity, the conflict with his father that leads to his mother's death, the betrayal by the princess, and the suffering he endures because of his split personality. With regard to the princess, the question is one of sincerity and loyalty. She is depicted as strong and valiant. When asked by the hedgehog whether she finds him very ugly, she responds, "Not so ugly as going back on a promise." Here she is referring to her father's promise, and we are introduced to another aspect of ugliness and beauty. Beauty is connected to loyalty, honesty, and respect, and later the princess feels ugly when she breaks her promise to the hedgehog not to reveal that he sheds his skin at night and is a handsome man. Swayed by her mother's false advice, the princess drives the hedgehog away, and she wears out three pairs of iron shoes on a long quest to find him. In the end, she must struggle with him so that he can regain his human form, and the tale ends with a second wedding, with the storyteller concluding, "This time the feasting went on for forty days and forty nights, and I myself was there to tell the best story there is to tell, a story that begins in hello and ends in goodbye, and for a gift they gave me a shoe worn to nothing. And here it is."

As the storyteller holds the shoe up, the dog shakes his head with skepticism, bringing the film to a close—but not really to a close, for the story has been questioned and may indeed have another version. In fact, at one point during the narration, the dog interrupts and insists that the storyteller is telling the story incorrectly. The dog shifts the narration according to his viewpoint until the storyteller picks up the threads and builds a role for himself within the narrative so that he is both inside and outside the narration. Throughout the film the narrative perspective keeps shifting through the interchange of the storyteller and the dog and through the artistic use of the camera, lighting, and sets.

The initial fireplace scene is the hearth of the stories, and out of the fire in darkness, the story unravels through the silhouettes of puppets behind a sheet, painted figures on a cracked antique plate, and finally the rural cottage in which the hedgehog is born. Live characters interact with puppets and fantastic creatures with no line drawn between reality and fantasy. The action moves from sets that imitate real homes and castles to canvas paintings of imaginary woods and hills. The surrealism of the images is heightened by slanted frames and camera shots taken from below. The cine-matic portrayal of the storyteller's tale is fabulous and filled with surprises so that the viewer is encouraged to expand his or her knowledge of storytelling and manner of looking at images. Even—or especially—if one is familiar with the Grimms' version of this beast/bridegroom tale, the film opens new insights into the tradi-tional scheme of things, exploring new artistic forms for conveying the themes of this particular tale.

All the films in *The Storyteller* series are creative experiments with classical tales, puppetry, cinematic techniques, painting, and music that reveal the potential of the film through television and video to recapture communal aspects of storytelling. Brought together in homes in front of a small screen, viewers see the story-teller actively engaged with a listener who interrupts, questions, mocks, laughs, and sighs while the story is told and enacted. A bond is formed between storyteller and listener and viewer, and the sharing of the story becomes a unique experience that does not call for identification or envelopment of the viewer.

Shelley Duvall's *Faerie Tale Theatre*

In an article that recorded Shelley Duvall's success as a television producer, *Forbes* reported, "In 1982 the pay television network Showtime, desperate for original programs to help it compete with both HBO and network TV, finally commissioned three *Faerie Tale Theatre* shows. Like most struggling business people, the first thing Duvall did was ask some of her friends—in this case Hollywood stars—for help, thereby bypassing the traditional channels of agents, managers and studios. Shrewdly targeting stars with children, Duvall asked for their help in creating quality television for kids."[11]

I must question the adjective *quality* in this article and whether the fairy-tale films were actually done for "kids." From 1984 to 1987, when *Faerie Tale Theatre* was sold into syndication, Duvall produced twenty-six episodes, each fifty minutes long, featuring Klaus Kinski and Susan Sarandon in "Beauty and the Beast," Dick Shawn, Art Carney, and Alan Arkin in "The Emperor's New Clothes," Eve Arden and Jean Stapleton in "Cinderella," Ben Vereen and Gregory Hines in "Puss in Boots," Lee Remick in "The

Snow Queen," Elizabeth McGovern, Vincent Price, and Vanessa Redgrave in "Snow White," Liza Minnelli and Tom Conti in "The Princess and the Pea," and Robin Williams and Terri Garr in "The Frog Prince," to name but a few of the star-studded productions.

Obviously, with actors like Redgrave, Remick, and Williams and directing by Eric Idle, Roger Vadim, and Duvall herself, the films had a certain professional "quality" to them, but the emphasis in most of the films was on the stars' tour-de-force performances rather than on re-creating the classical fairy tales in an innovative manner. Spectacle, amusement for the sake of the actors' obvious enjoyment and for amusement's own sake, and simplistic renarrating of the traditional plots that are merely touched up with ornaments are some of the "quality" features of *Faerie Tale Theatre*, and yet amid its glitter and pomp there are some stimulating films. Duvall's policy was one of laissez-faire, so there are many different cinematic styles and interpretations of the fairy tales.

For example, the productions of "Red Riding Hood" and "Beauty and the Beast," directed by Roger Vadim, are indicative of the retrogressive quality of the entire series. Though Malcolm McDowell is amusing in his role as the bungling wolf, the portrayal of Red Riding Hood and her relationship to her father is so infantile, blatantly oedipal, and stupid that the story is reduced to a tract denouncing female gullibility and celebrating male power. The setting and the characterization are one-dimensional and read or view no better than a cheap storybook version that one can buy in a supermarket. "Beauty and the Beast" is not much better. Vadim offers us a slavish imitation of Jean Cocteau's famous *La Belle et la Bête* but without its sophistication, and there is no endeavor to re-create the story line or add to the characterization, as the Disney Studios did in its animated version of *Beauty and the Beast*. Everything is predictable in the film and thus boring, and it is difficult to comprehend why Beauty would want to sacrifice herself for her father or the beast, despite Klaus Kinski's fine acting.

In contrast to these stale imitations of the classical fairy tales, Eric Idle's production of "The Frog Prince" is a superb adaptation because it is a hilarious parody that makes unusual artistic use of puppets and masks. In Idle's script, the story opens with a curse placed on a baby prince by an old crone who was not invited to his christening because the forgetful queen did not think she would fit in well with the courtly society. Of course the queen and king are aghast to find their son turned into a frog, but there is nothing they can do about it. Many years pass, and we are introduced to another royal household in which an extremely vain princess terrorizes the servants and her parents. Played to perfection by Terri Garr, this princess is so excessively haughty that she is ridiculous—even the servants make fun of her. Once she loses her golden ball, given to her by "an adolescent prince with homicidal tendencies," she strikes a deal with a talking frog, played by Robin Williams, who is the voice of an adroit green puppet. Of course, the princess breaks her promise and calls the frog a sucker. When the frog pursues her, he is almost cooked by a French chef but is saved by the king, who is afraid of disorder and revolution and thus wants his daughter to keep her promise. The frog turns out to be a charmer at the king's feast; he dances, sings, tells jokes, and does a Shakespeare routine. When the princess retires for the evening, she is compelled to take him with her. Then, to her surprise, he defends her with sword in hand against an ugly insect. She softens and rewards him with a kiss. All at once, the frog turns into a naked prince, covered only by a towel. Attracted to each other, the princess and prince begin kissing again to see how the charm works. But then the king arrives and refuses to believe that the prince was once a frog. So the prince is thrown into prison, and the princess is sent to a strict boarding school. Later, the old crone who started everything appears to the king in a golden ball and reveals the truth, so the king pardons the prince and arranges for a marriage. The crone promises that will be the end of her frog tricks, but there is a great deal of doubt whether this promise will be fulfilled.

Like the Muppet film of *The Frog Prince*, this film subverts the traditional story line to stimulate the viewer to question the old fairy-tale lines. The language is American slang, and there are numerous sexual innuendos that charge the film with exciting and comical erotic play. Most of the characters undergo change in the course of action, and the puppetry, music, and sets are designed to enhance the humor of the narration. The cinematic portrayal of the monarchy and court life is clearly critical of the pomposity of royalty and arbitrary use of power. In the process, the beast/bridegroom tale is no longer about the self-sacrifice of a woman who is obliged to save a bestial man but about vanity, hypocrisy, and the power of humor to expose false consciousness.

Aside from "The Frog Prince," there are other films in the *Faerie Tale Theatre* series such as "The Three Little Pigs" and "Jack and the Beanstalk" that are innovative adaptations of classical fairy tales and other fairy-tale films. However, without a clear educational or philosophical policy, the films are hit-or-miss commodities that may or may not contribute to the creative and critical awareness of young viewers.

Tom Davenport

If there is little systematic thought and thorough reflection behind the philosophical and production policies of Duvall's *Faerie Tale Theatre*, the opposite may be said of Tom Davenport's remarkable adaptations of the Grimms' fairy tales for young audiences. An independent filmmaker, Davenport has carefully elaborated his ideas about exploring fairy tales and folk traditions in films since 1975, and in a recent article about filmmaking, "Making Grimm Movies," he discussed how his new three-part film series about fairy-tale adaptations is intended to develop the creative potential of his young viewers: "Because film and television have become the primary bearers of myth and storytelling (and, consequently the charter for social action in our country), understanding how to make film and video will empower people who may otherwise feel helpless and manipulated by media. Some teachers are already accepting video reports from students who are eager to explore the power of camcorder, VCR, and computer. Once people begin to understand how the film and television are made, they will fear it less and respect it more."[12] Indeed, his current work in fairy-tale adaptation for the screen shows a steady progression in innovative experimentation and his concern in educating children about fairy tales and film.

Relying mainly on grants from the National Endowment for the Arts, the Public Broadcasting Service, and other foundations to further his explorative work, Davenport has collaborated with actors, technicians, storytellers, and writers to bring out essential psychological and social features of the Grimms' tales in his films and printed versions that are directly related to folklore. He has not "modernized" the tales in a slick, sensationalist manner. Rather, he has historicized the tales and carefully shifted the focus by giving them American settings from the seventeenth century to the present.[13] By introducing American characters and events in American history, he has shown how such qualities as patience, cunning, and courage help his protagonists overcome poverty, prejudice, and hardship during wars, famine, and depression. Davenport is interested in how people survive oppression, particularly how they survive with pride and a sense of their own dignity. Through his films he conveys these "fairy tales of survival" to give young viewers a sense of hope, especially at a time in American history when violence, poverty, and degradation appear to minimize their hope for a better future.

The first three films, *Hansel and Gretel* (1975), *Rapunzel* (1979), and *The Frog King* (1980), which Davenport coproduced with his wife, Mimi, were all set in the South and Appalachia and are period pieces. Most of the shooting was done on location, with close attention paid to typical customs, architecture, landscape, and dialects. The difficulty with these films is that Davenport relied too closely on the plots of the Grimms' tales. For instance, while *The Frog King* is an obvious attempt to re-create the conditions of antebellum life in the South, there are some racist and sexist implications in its depiction of the servants and the princess. Davenport changed the setting of the German tale, but he reproduced the story line that involves the humiliation of the princess (the traditional taming-of-the-shrew theme) and celebration of male rule. In his early work, Davenport had not yet learned to use folklore and history critically so that more liberating alternatives to oppressive situations could be explored.

However, since the production of *Jack and the Dentist's Daughter* (1983), an original adaptation of an Appalachian folk tale with black characters—one of the only fairy-tale films ever produced with ethnic minority characters as protagonists—Davenport has made original use of the fairy tale and film to enhance viewers' understanding of storytelling, politics, and creativity. One of his best endeavors is his 1990 film *Ashpet: An American Cinderella.* This cinematic version is about a young white woman named Lily, who learns to reclaim her rights and heritage through the help of a wise black woman whose sense of history and knowledge of oppression empowers the "enslaved" Lily to pursue her dreams. The action takes place in the rural South during the early years of World War II, when people were making sacrifices and being forced

Ashpet: An American Cinderella. Reprinted by permission of Davenport Films.

to separate because of the military draft. But Lily manages to find
the strength to overcome isolation and exploitation by piecing
together a sense of her own story, which her stepmother and step-
sisters had taken from her. Consequently, Davenport's Cinderella
story is no longer history in a traditional male sense, that is, no
longer the Grimms' tale or a simple rags-to-riches story. Nor is it a
didactic feminist interpretation. Instead, Davenport turns it into
an American tale about conflict within a matrilineal heritage in

Ashpet: An American Cinderella. Reprinted by permission of Davenport Films.

the South, narrated from beginning to end by a well-known Afro-American storyteller, Louise Anderson, who plays the role of Dark Sally, the magical conjure-woman and fairy godmother. Dark Sally becomes the focus of the film, which shows how her storytelling can lead a young woman to recover a sense of her history and give her the strength to assert herself, as many women are doing today.

The fairy tale as historical document and history as fairy tale are two premises with which Davenport works in all his films. Since his training was in documentary filmmaking, it is not by chance that these films have a unique quality of reportage, as though they were newsreels from the past. Davenport works closely with historians, folklorists, artists, storytellers, and actors to develop a sense of historical authenticity that does not undermine the magic of the fairy tales. Paradoxically, the fantastic occurrences in the film have more impact because of their historical foundation.

In addition to using history and the fairy tale to shed light on social developments and the nature of storytelling, Davenport has published newsletters about each film that are made available to schools. These newsletters are pedagogical tools intended to help teachers and students explore and understand the films in their present context and to go beyond them.[14] In this manner, Davenport demonstrates that he has learned from the responses to his films and tries to incorporate these lessons into each new production.[15]

Conclusion

As the work of Henson, Duvall, and Davenport reveals, filmmakers have indeed gone beyond Disney in the adaptation of fairy tales for the screen,[16] and one could point to other interesting fairy-tale films such as Rob Reiner's *The Princess Bride* (1987), Ralph Bakshi's *Wizards* (1977), Wolfgang Petersen's *The NeverEnding Story* (1984), or television series such as *The Fractured Fairy Tales* (1961–1964).[17] Indeed, in one of the more pointed and hilarious cartoons, *Sleeping Beauty*, the handsome prince is a caricature of Walt Disney, and when he discovers Sleeping Beauty, he withholds his magic kiss and builds an amusement park around her called Sleeping Beautyland to make money. The evil fairy wants a cut of the profits, and Walt the Prince tries various ways to have her eliminated. After all, Disney never wanted to share or have anyone try to go beyond him, but this fractured fairy tale exposes him and demonstrates through its clever humor and animation that there are ways to transcend Disney.

Keeping things in perspective, we must remember that Disney was in fact a pioneer in that he pointed out the great possibilities animation and film had for the effective expansion of the fairy-tale genre into the age of mechanical reproduction. However, instead of fully realizing those possibilities, he became absorbed in their commodification after establishing the fairy-tale film as art form.

Just what is the potential of the fairy-tale film as art form and ideological expression, already realized in part in the works I have discussed? How can fairy-tale films further the autonomy of young viewers and stimulate their creative and critical faculties?

Children are exposed to the social design of reality from the moment they are born. Adult versions of "reality" are imposed upon children to ensure that they are positioned physically, socially, and culturally to experience their own growth and life around them in specified ways. "Reality" is held up to them as empirically verifiable and as an inexorable force. Fairy tales have always balanced and subverted this process and offered the possibility of seeing reality as an illusion. As children become aware of the artifices and machinations in their lives, they gain the sense of alternatives for making their own lives more meaningful and pleasurable. Thus, through the cinematic adaptations of fairy tales reality can be displayed as artificiality so that children can develop a sense of assembling and reassembling the frames of their lives for themselves.

Going beyond Disney is therefore the realization that fairy tales do not begin and end with Disney and that one can make one's own life resemble a fairy tale that transcends antiquated notions of patriarchy and racism. Going beyond Disney means realizing that there are no prescriptions for fairy tales or for happiness. To paraphrase a famous quotation from the German romantic writer Novalis—"Menschwerden ist eine Kunst"—learning how to become a compassionate human being involves learning to live life as an artist—and, I might add, learning to transform our fairy-tale dreams into narratives of our own making.

5

Lion Kings
and the Culture Industry

It has been over half a century since Max Horkheimer and Theodor Adorno published *Dialectic of Enlightenment*. With the passage of time and the continual commodification of culture in America, it seems appropriate to review some of Horkheimer and Adorno's major theses of the concept of the culture industry to see how they have weathered the cultural debates and the rise of postmodernism in the 1980s and 1990s, when daily life has become so overwhelmingly aestheticized that the particular meanings of community and individual identity have lost all significance. Such a loss allows for the shaping of ethnic and national identities purported to be deeply inbred in their members along with false religious traditions that politicians exploit to increase their power within a system that they cannot really control.

Adorno knew—and I am focusing mainly on Adorno because he, unlike Horkheimer, continued to explore all aspects of the culture industry until his death—that the collapse of the division between high and low art would lead to greater violence and the spectacle of victimization. *Dialectic of Enlightenment* was generated not only by Adorno's experiences with German fascism but also, and perhaps more significantly, by his encounters with American capitalism of the 1930s and 1940s. Almost all the examples that Adorno used in his writings on the culture industry are related to developments in the United States or developments that originated there, and he continued to follow and critique these examples until his death in 1969. There is a long passage from "On the Fetish Character in Music and the Regression of Listening" that cuts right to the core of his concern:

> The concept of musical fetishism cannot be psychologically derived. That 'values' are consumed and draw feelings to themselves, without their specific qualities being reached by the consciousness of the consumer, is a later expression of their commodity character. For all contemporary musical life is dominated by the commodity form; the last pre-capitalist residues have been eliminated. Music, with all the attributes of the ethereal and sublime which are generously accorded it, serves in America today as an advertisement for commodities which one must acquire in order to be able to hear music. If the advertising function is carefully dimmed in the case of serious music, it always breaks through in the case of light music. The whole jazz business, with its free distribution of scores to bands, has abandoned the idea that actual performance promotes the sale of piano scores and phonograph records. Countless hit song texts praise the hit songs themselves, repeating the titles in capital letters. What makes its appearance, like an idol, out of such masses of type is the exchange value in which the quantum of possible enjoyment has disappeared.[1]

What happens with music also occurs in all other domains of art and leisure. Adorno went on to remark that the consumer appears to be in an immediate relationship with the goods, and it is this *appearance* that gives cultural goods their exchange value. Adorno stated, "The feelings which go to the exchange value create the appearance of immediacy at the same time as the absence of a relation to the object belies it. It has its basis in the abstract character of exchange values. Every 'psychological' aspect, every ersatz satisfaction, depends on such social substitution. The change in the function of music involves the basic conditions of the relation between art and society. The more inexorably the principle of exchange value destroys use values for human beings, the more deeply does exchange value disguise itself as the object of enjoyment."[2]

More pessimistic than Walter Benjamin, Adorno believed that totalitarianism would spread in capitalist societies through the mass reproduction of art and exchange values determined by capitalist commodification in all spheres of life. Since all forms of interaction and mediation have come to be based on appearance, or what Benjamin called the aestheticization of politics, Adorno argued that the culture industry would ultimately be key in stamping not only the "quality" of art but the very essence of individual autonomy. Here is, another important Adorno quotation:

> The masochistic mass culture is the necessary manifestation of almighty production itself. When the feelings seize on exchange value it is no mystical transubstantiation. It corresponds to the behaviour of the prisoner who loves his cell because he has been left nothing else to love. The sacrifice of individuality, which accommodates itself to the regularity of the successful, the doing of what everybody does, follows from the basic fact that in broad areas the same thing is offered to everybody by the standardized production of consumption goods. But the commercial necessity of connecting this identity leads to the manipulation of taste and the official culture's pretense of individualism which necessarily increases in proportion to the liquidation of the individual.[3]

For Adorno, the entry fee into any Western capitalist society, if one wanted success, was the surrender of individualism, and art's role was to manipulate listeners and viewers to identify with stars, to take pleasure from such identification, and to seek power through identification with star commodities. In his analyses of film, sport, theater, radio, and television, Adorno consistently focused on the operative and instrumental means by which the culture industry generated modes of production and behavior involving the complicity of the masses. Individuality had to be willingly abandoned for imitation of stereotypical stars emanating power, who were themselves products of the culture industry. Often labeled an elitist by his critics because he denounced the conformity of mass behavior and mass culture, Adorno actually wrote on behalf of the so-called masses, for he wanted to make everyone aware of what the masses have become and to prompt his readers *not* to succumb to the culture industry. In short, Adorno spoke out on behalf of individuality, originality, uniqueness, and particularism. Although he defended high art, or what he also called responsible art, Adorno never aligned such art with a particular class, nor did he celebrate the "high" or upper classes as chosen people, elected to show the truthful way to the proper goals of life through art. As far as he was concerned, anyone could belong to the masses, and practically everyone did even while believing that they were distinct and original entities. Here, of course, was the problem: the capacity of the culture industry to make masses of people believe that they were unique, different, and original while compelling them to conform to market conditions and subscribe to political systems whose major role was to explore every possible way to endorse and spread the capitalist production of commodities.

Unfortunately, with few exceptions, Adorno's ideas have not been used to examine and counter the manner in which socialization of children takes place in the United States. The entertainment industry (toys, games, books, films, advertising, videocassettes, television) begins to influence infants soon after they are born, and commercial firms have successfully entered schools, private and public, not merely to sell their products but to induce children to learn about selling themselves as products and to emulate stars through the adoption of masochistic attitudes. David Denby has lamented, "Aided by armies of psychologists and market researchers, the culture industries reach my children at every stage of their desires and their inevitable discontent. What's lost is the old dream that parents and teachers will nurture the organic development of the child's own nature. That dream is largely dead. In this country, people possessed solely by the desire to sell have become far more powerful than parents tortuously working out the contradictions of authority, freedom, education, and soul-making."4

The focus in education, as Herbert Marcuse long ago pointed out, is still on achievement, yet achievement involves surrendering personal desires or the shaping of libidinal energy and molding oneself to be popular and successful. In the United States even if one is not or cannot be "number one," one is motivated as a child to identify with the star or team that is. Kids play with dolls, guns, games, robots, books, and computers that allegedly give them a sense of power and confidence.

Marsha Kinder has demonstrated how theater, video, films, and screenplays are made to imbue children with a false sense of power.[5] She shows how Saturday morning television shows, video games, and films help form a gendered subject who is supposed to believe that he or she can develop protean powers to appropriate the world and buy his or her way into a world more concerned with commodities than with people. Of course, the boy or girl subjects have clearly delineated gender roles, the more adventurous and powerful ones for the boys and the cheerleading and decorative ones for the girls. Though children do develop some cognitive skills through television, movies, and video games, they also "imbibe" a false sense of power and aggressive instincts that further competition in a capitalist market system. Whatever skills are gained through television, movies, and videos are gained at the expense of humanitarian values. Though the narratives of the various television shows, movies, and videos may seem to differ, they all tend to homogenize child viewers through narrative constructs that frame their lives as "precocious consumers." There are few antidotes to commercial television, movies, and videos, and Kinder's study does not argue for abolishing these media. In fact, the best way to oppose the negative impact of such media narratives is to work with them and reutilize the media to create different values and a social awareness that leads to more responsible autonomy. What's called for are children and adults with discriminating minds.

Is it really possible to work within the institutions of the culture industry to change it? Perhaps, but such work must be undertaken with a recognition of the limitations set by the industry and the capitalist system as they assume new global forms. Here Paul Piccone's category of "artificial negativity" is useful, for he demonstrated in a series of articles that Western states did not have to resort to fascism or overt coercion in order to maintain the capitalist system.[6] Indeed, capitalism had already exceeded Adorno's worst prognosis because it could co-opt and needed an image of originality and uniqueness to legitimate the "free market" and the "democratic" political system in forms of artificial negativity. In 1978 Piccone wrote,

> In order for the system to function, it needs control mechanisms such as the Naders and the Commoners to guarantee its viability. Far from being persecuted, the lingering opposition now needs to be supported to keep functional a bureaucracy in a state of fatal involution. Counter-bureaucratic bureaucracies become one of the paradoxical expressions of artificially generated negativity. The problem with this system-generated negativity is that, to the extent that it is itself bureaucratically sanctioned, it tends to become an extension of the very bureaucracy in need of control. Consequently, caught in the paperwork of funding, reporting, justifying, etc., it simply extends the bureaucratic logic it was meant to challenge and becomes counter-productive.[7]

Although Piccone did not analyze the culture industry in what he called the new phase of capitalism, he did claim that capitalism can sustain itself only through cultural hegemony. Given the tendency of the system to overproduce and underconsume, the thrust toward economic crisis can be averted only by successfully disposing of the surplus and exporting the ecological problems generated by intensified production.

What is crucial for the United States at this point is the guarantee that international trade will continue to grow. The logic of "unequal exchange," whereby any trade between a more advanced country and a less developed one will result in the former having the upper hand, not only places the United States in a favorable economic situation but also allows for the exportation of the resulting ecological problems. Increasingly, less developed countries will be able to offer the United States in trade precisely those items (usually natural resources) whose continued extraction or manufacture raises ecological questions. Thus, according to Piccone, the system's Achille's heel is no longer economic, social, or political but *cultural*—and at this level there are no challenges anywhere except perhaps in Southern Europe. As long as consumerism is not seriously challenged by the simultaneous demystifying of technocratic management, scientific ideologies, and hierarchical relations in everyday life and by the general raising of questions about quality of life and *meaning*, capitalism will thrive—short of a global ecological catastrophe (but this possibility remains so remote at present, and postponable by technological means, that it is not yet a realistic prospect).[8]

We can forget the potential cultural challenge of Southern Europe—Piccone wrote this essay in 1978. But we cannot forget Piccone's warning about the spread of consumerism and the manner in which it is maintained, in part, through artificial negativity.

The fall of the Berlin Wall in 1989 has been a great prop for capitalism in our so-called postmodern era. Consumerism has spread like a tidal wave over the former Soviet Union and has inundated China as well. Along with the spread of the consumer mentality, the "free" market of capitalism has brought with it greater violence, crime, and unemployment and allegedly greater cultural forms of freedom of expression that are plugged into the culture industry throughout Eastern Europe. At the same time, the postmodernist practices of artists and intellectuals of every stripe have "countered" the culture industry and have supposedly developed subversive and emancipatory alternatives through the eclectic combination of high and low art in everyday life. Through parody, exaggeration, repulsion, and indiscrimination, postmodern culture has offered some moments of protest and resistance to the culture industry, but in the long run even those moments are really an expression or a manifestation of the desperate situation in which most people find themselves today, whether they have privileged access to the "system" or are oppressed by it. J. M. Bernstein has pointed out that the culture industry has easily made use of the postmodernist "challenge" to capitalism. Indeed, postmodern art is actually more an extension and product of the culture industry than anything else, or another form of artificial negativity. Bernstein states,

Without the constraint of form, which dictated the path of subli-
mation, desublimated desires find themselves set against the same
illusory comforts and real obstacles to happiness as precipitated the
need for desublimation in the first instance. The culture industry's
response is the production of works, typified in the new architecture, that, through a mimesis of aestheticization, indict the specta-
tor for failing to find gratification where there is none. The release
from the rigours of form into the apparent utopian play of differences should have produced a sublime release from the repressions
of everyday life under capital and the only illusory dynamic of high
culture. Instead, the postmodern sublime (the sublime defeat of the
a priori of closed forms), through its aggressive insistence on overcoming the divide between high and low, and integrating art and
empirical life, perpetuates the sublime's violent repression of desire
without the concomitant moment of release. By this route postmodernism's presumptive affirmation, by offering what is repression
as satisfaction, makes the moment of self-negation permanent and
thus an intended celebration of death. Because postmodernist practice alters the empirical world without transforming it, its abstract
affirmations belie the despair that sustains it. That despair manifests
itself in aggression and violence, a violence now represented,
exploited and celebrated in the media. The violence perpetuated by
instrumental reason on sensuous particularity, what Adorno terms
the 'non-identical,' is answered only with violence.[9]

Clearly, it is the function of present postmodern culture to decorate,
embellish, and alter our everyday experiences without qualitatively
changing the conditions of the world around us. Politicians, artists,
and intellectuals are all involved in the business of damage control.
Since there is no real threat to capitalism, the conflicts in the world
center around which groups will have the right and power to man-
age capitalism as it spreads and goes through crises. What group of
managers will be most efficient, and how can they best make use of
the culture industry without resorting to outright force to placate
contending interest groups in the present world constellation? Violence and victimization will of course continue to exist at a high
level in daily life because they are necessary for legitimating the

state and the state bureaucracy. Outright violence such as totalitarian police measures and war will be necessary only when the culture industry breaks down, and there are no signs that such a breakdown will occur. Today the focus is primarily on globalization and global economies, but it may be more important to analyze how this capitalist globalization is reinforced through the culture industry, which affects socialization on a global scale. The following personal anecdotes, which I have culled from recent trips to Europe and travels around the United States, exemplify this dynamic.

Looking Artificially at Europe as Flaneur

When I was a student in Europe some thirty years ago, it was easy for Europeans to recognize me as an American because of the clothes I wore, my gait, my movements. Now, however, I am one of the crowd—anonymous. Everyone dresses like Americans, and Americans dress like everyone else. There are Adidas, Nike, Timberland labels on everyone's shoes. Sweatshirts and shirts advertise their manufacturers. Even umbrellas and coats have a logo of some kind. We are all walking advertisements, just as all of the tennis players and soccer stars in the world along with their stadiums are now beacons of advertising. But clothes and logos by themselves do not make people; there are also gestures and movements and other decorations to consider. So I watch how young students imitate actors on popular television shows influenced by dubbed American sitcoms and films, and I see them gesticulate and move like Americans. (Or do Americans move like Europeans?) The hip among them have rings in their ears, noses, and lips. Their American baseball hats are on backward. The sweaters stick out from under their jackets that are bound to advertise something. Their jeans are worn out. I watch the older people who also model themselves after lookalike ads that I have seen throughout Europe and America, and I look like them as I walk, secure in my anonymity.

As an American in Europe, I watch as the French police in the Metro and on the streets of Paris stop only people of color, question them, search them, and perhaps arrest them, just as these events may occur in Berlin, London, or Minneapolis on a daily basis. Everyone not involved tries to ignore this scene—it is for our safety—because we know through films and television that we need protection from terrorists, criminals, and tyrants. Wherever I go in Europe, I know I can turn on a television set and watch the same types of news broadcasts, shows, and films in a certain sequence. It does not matter what language the characters are speaking. Their voices have the same authoritative tone. They are all look-alikes, as are their gestures and movements. I can also walk into any theater or movie theater to see a serious classical play, an exciting new drama, or the latest Disney hit film and find that the culture industry has systematically ordered the daily offerings, sequence of presentations, and contents.

Looking at Disney's *The Lion King* in Florence, Italy

Actually, you do not have to turn to the newspapers and mass media to learn about terrorism and tyrants or about the pervasiveness of the culture industry. One Disney film provides a way to grasp where we are and what we are supposed to think and feel. Disney films and products are everywhere in Europe, just as most American fast-food chains have taken hold in Europe. But it does not matter whether American products take root in Europe or European and Asian products swamp American markets. They are very much the same; only the wrappers differ. The labels and advertisements tell us that our lives can become different and more glorious as they repeat the same scenes with new gadgets, tricks, colors, and movements.

Disney Studios is a master at bringing feature films of our lives into our homes. But my daughter and I, in one instance, went out to see *Le Re Leone* (*The Lion King*) at a local movie house at the Piazza Beccheria in Florence. It was Christmas Eve, 1994. The movie house was packed with munching and gabbing children and parents. Nothing is sacred anymore on holy holidays—even in Catholic countries. Local advertisements flashed on the screen as everyone tried to get comfortable. Then came the previews, mixed with more but slicker advertisements. Finally, *The Lion King* rolled across the screen: thunderous music and animals moving in a procession to admire the birth of a new lion prince named Simba. High on a cliff overlooking a vast plain, Simba is held in the air next to his glorious blond-furred parents. The multicultural animals bow reverentially, and the sun shines brightly on this scene. Yet we know (from previous Disney films) that this happy order must be challenged, so we are introduced to the king's brother, a dark-featured lion with a black mane of hair (what else?), who associates with ridiculous-looking laughing hyenas who inhabit dark places with skeletons strewn about the ground. The evil brother (who is actually portrayed as Hitler in one scene) plots the murder of Simba, and eventually, with the help of the hyenas (the SS troops), he manages to kill his brother and place the blame on Simba, who believes that he is responsible for his father's death.

Little Simba runs off in shame and eventually finds himself in another realm, the jungle, where he meets two weird friends, a boar and a gopher; grows into a huge lion; and enjoys the comforts of a jungle paradise. Meanwhile, the evil uncle has ravaged the former kingdom, and only by chance does Simba learn that his kingdom has been devastated. His former playmate, now a beautiful lioness, wanders into the jungle in chase of the boar and finds him. She and a wise old monkey, who is also a karate expert and guru, convince him to return and claim his throne. Of course, Simba does return and leads a magnificent battle among thunder, rain, fire, cliffs, ravines, and caves. Everyone joins in, and naturally, Simba triumphs while the hyenas eat the evil uncle (off the screen, of course). The final scene repeats the first scene, with Simba's lioness giving birth to a cub and the wise monkey exhibiting it on a cliff to the reverent multicultural animals. The perfect frame as the celebration of the status quo. The eternal return of the same.

My daughter loved this film. My daughter loves all the Disney films. At age four, though I had sworn that it would be forbidden in my house, she was given her first Barbie doll, and there was no stopping the flood after that. At age eleven, she now has twenty or more Barbie dolls without genitals (just as the animals in the Disney film have no genitals), and these dolls with their perfect figures and features can do anything. They can even act out the Disney films, television films, Space Rangers shows, or other popular programs that she watches. She knows whatever is popular as toy, film, game, dress. She learns about it in school, on television, in movie theaters, or in talks with her friends.

Why did my daughter love *The Lion King?* I asked her because I have tried to introduce her to other types of fairy tales and other types of art. She could not tell me exactly why except that she found the animals cute and charming. She felt sorry when the king died. She felt glad when Simba returned and became king again. My daughter has good reasons for liking the film, though she also likes "good" films and literature. She knows how to like it because she has received commodity training in taste despite my questions and objections. On the other hand, I sit through the movie horrified. I wonder how much of the politics of the film will seep into her brain. How much will she be encouraged to worship and admire some male king? How much will she want to become a star and stand on a cliff before multitudes of reverent people? Whether she joins the masses below or aspires to become the lioness or lion on top of the cliff, it is all repulsive to me.

Looking at Other Lion Kings

But I do not have to go to the cinema to be repulsed by lion king ideas. Whatever I read, wherever I travel, whatever I watch, there are lion kings who promise to restore order to ravaged kingdoms or to maintain order so that their subjects can continue to consume in peace without the threat of outsiders taking their jobs and lives. The media paint political conflicts by celebrating or deprecating lion kings: What we need are good leaders. Rarely do I read political analyses of the systems that produce the leaders. Every report and show focuses on political leaders who are either victimizing their people or their country or being victimized. When I was in Italy in 1995, Silvio Berlusconi claimed to have been victimized by the media that allegedly damaged his chances to become prime minister, even though he controlled most of the important television stations. In the United States, Bill Clinton has lost power by the devastating defeat of his forces in Congress, and he is now seeking to regain the confidence of the American people, who rarely vote, perhaps because they realize how useless it is in a system geared to make fools of them. Despite corruption and scandals, John Major has retained power in Great Britain, as Helmut Kohl has in Germany, for their economies are strong enough *not* to legitimize a change. This is the case in France too, where Jacques Chirac has assumed autocratic control. However, all of these kings are names representative of exchange values, and the kings can be exchanged—and some will have been by the time this book is published—without damage to market forces and political systems. They are there to exhibit their talents as damage controllers, and they will be exchanged only when *certain* interest groups decide that the state and economy need more efficient control. Cost efficiency is the name of the game today.

Looking at Controlled Sports

Control in the name of civility and civilization is what the world is about, and control of the culture industry enables lion kings to gain and keep control. Spontaneity is out, though we all long for it, desire it, miss it. Control is the name of the game.

In Europe, where soccer is king, the masses must be controlled at games. Stadiums have become Roman coliseums with barbed wire and guards patrolling them inside and outside. The contests on the fields are secondary to the event of going to the stadium and participating in the hoped-for victory. It is important to be number one, to win at all costs. Such outright display of ruthless desire goes against the rules of civility, and thus it must be contained and controlled, just as rock concerts are carefully planned and controlled. Sports are spectacle, but a controlled spectacle, in which people can briefly vent their frustration according to a prescribed rite. Now and then people are unfortunately killed, trampled on, or beaten, either for revenge or because the celebration gets out of hand. Such catastrophes prompt greater control and stronger police measures. But the spectacle, almost like artificial negativity, is nonetheless necessary.

In 1994, in America, soccer journalists and fans were surprised that there were few police and dogs at the World Cup matches and that there was no barbed wire or moat surrounding the playing fields. It appears that sporting events are much more civilized in America, and for the most part they are. Anywhere and everywhere you go in America, from organized baseball games for "peewees" to professional football games, such events are the same and are becoming more and more the same. Even the outcome of the game is predictably the same before you enter a stadium—if you can afford a ticket.

Recently I went to a Minnesota Timberwolves basketball game with a friend. Although this team is one of the worst in the National Basketball Association, I could not spontaneously get a ticket and go to the game because the tickets were sold out before the season began, mainly to rich season subscribers or scalpers. But my friend had connections, and we went to the Target Center, an arena built four years ago with the latest high-tech designs. It was the first *live* basketball game I had seen in about twenty years, and I was stunned.

As I entered the Target Center, there were stands and sellers everywhere with colored neon lights flickering on and off to attract the attention of the spectators. Enormous quantities of junk food and junk products were being sold, all advertising the Timberwolves or some other team or product. Once we were inside the arena, vendors kept coming through the aisles before, during, and after the game. The consumption of food was continuous. Sexy female cheerleaders, all much too old to be cheerleaders yet cheerleaders nevertheless, tried to drum up support for *their* team through dance routines copied from Broadway musicals. An acrobatic mascot, a man dressed as a timberwolf, did all sorts of leaps and capers on the floor to divert the crowd before the game began. Once the teams had warmed up, the lights were turned off. Then music blared as each one of the starting five players was introduced with a spotlight shining on the star. Finally, the national anthem was announced, and the crowd stood and faced a huge, draped American flag. "The Star-Spangled Banner" was sung by some celebrity as many spectators placed their hands on their hearts. Above the crowd, in the middle of the arena, was a huge scoreboard and television set framed by changing neon advertisements. Everyone, including the players, could see the action on the screen better than they could from their places, and many did watch the game on the television screen while it was in progress.

The game was incidental to the event filled with all sorts of sideshows: the giggling cheerleaders constantly changing costumes to attract attention during their routines; the vendors shouting humorous refrains to draw the buyer's attention; the timberwolf mascot jumping off a trampoline and dunking the ball to amaze the spectators; a contest between spectators at halftime to see if they could make half-court shots; one of the players spitting on an assistant coach; fans seeking autographs; players giving interviews.

The game was boring because it was essentially controlled by the coaches. There are multiple set plays in basketball now that are always called by the coach. The timeouts are determined by the timing of television advertisements, the referees, and the coaches as part of the controlling strategy. Throughout the game, the coaches decide whom to substitute and what to do in any given situation. Though the players are the star performers, it is actually the coach of the team, who jumps up and down on the bench and demands the attention of his players, referees, and spectators, who is the real celebrity, the lion king who will save the game with his calls. There are lion kings everywhere who are called upon to save the game and the kingdom, to make the team number one, and bring glory to the nation. Even universities have their lion kings.

Looking at the University

During the past twenty years I have taught at four different universities, private and public, and the situation has always been the same. The president, provosts, and deans have constantly struggled to obtain more money from the board of regents or trustees and to keep costs down. The faculty are exploited and pitted against the deans, former professors who identify with the institution as administrators. The faculty wants more self-governance, larger salaries, and money to develop programs. The students complain that they are not getting enough for their money and that there are no jobs for them when they are ready to enter "the market." In the meantime, everyone talks about the "quality" of education becoming worse, and political correctness as one of the major contributing factors to the deterioration of the university.

The answer to the problems of rising costs, poor teaching and scholarship, unemployment for graduate students, and rabid radicalism at campuses in the form of political correctness and multiculturalism is, of course, a new president who will better control things and bring about reforms. One of the reforms is to change or eliminate tenure so that professors will learn to toe the company line. Another is to eliminate programs that are not productive or do not entice students, often referred to as customers. Lion-king presidents and deans these days talk about cost-efficient programs and close down entire programs and branches of universities because they are not bringing in money and their market value is not high enough to justify sustaining them. So presidents (with the approval of the regents and state legislature) cut positions and stop hiring new candidates. They constantly ask departments to review their programs, even though the programs may be working very well. They institute new rules and regulations and create so much paperwork that professors have little time to concentrate on teaching and scholarship. There are meetings to discuss further meetings. There are speeches about what must be done to reform the university. Everything must be on the mend. In the meantime, fees are raised for the students, who have larger classes and fewer professors.

Most presidents and deans of colleges and universities are compelled to make such changes to meet market conditions and to create "lean, mean machines." Very rarely do they resist the regents and trustees. Rather, they make compromises that will enable them to stay in power and to address the outside needs of the state and culture industry within the university itself. There is very little space for resistance or protest at the university because everyone is consumed by paperwork, trying to salvage something from the constant reordering that has nothing to do with education.

Looking at Artificial Negativity

As I watch myself at the university, I realize how much I contribute to maintaining the status quo. Whatever protest element I have tried to introduce in my teaching, writing, and outside activities has eventually been co-opted to legitimize the tolerance and democracy of the institution. It would seem that the only effective and authentic means of protest must come from outside, from the margins of the system, in order to undermine the consumer mentality. The long march through the institutions to change them has proved to be illusory and self-deluded.

Yet outside protest is also illusory, and what is real is the culture industry, which has expanded to the point of monopolizing all areas of art, sport, education, and so on. Its tentacles are everywhere and are too many to ever (at least in our lifetime) be completely cut off. The culture industry itself was a *necessary* development, closely connected to technological progress, the demands of the capitalist free market for greater profits, the rise of literacy, the advance of mechanical reproduction, and the desire of masses of people to lead better and happier lives. Though it is seemingly omnipotent, there are, of course, contradictions in the culture industry that open gaps in people's lives, and not all negativity is artificially produced. There are real needs that supply force to negativity. In 1978 Piccone saw the Achilles' heel of present-day capitalism as cultural, and today his major focus is on the reconception and reconstruction, if not recuperation, of communal life, something he claims is happening everywhere though I do not see these signs. Rather, I see the encroachment of the culture industry in all communities, large and small. Such encroachment will not stop unless the protest movements focus their energies more on the early education of children and radical changes of family relations and the manner in which power takes shape and is used in families and communities. In her book *Children First*, Penelope Leach has argued that children will not learn to think critically or to organize around their own interests unless the community is reshaped to provide early childhood centers and more effective child care by men and women who come together in support of children's welfare. At present children are either *massively* neglected in Western society or socialized according to the needs of the culture industry. Books, toys, shows, plays, games, food, clothing, and centers are produced to give them a sense of how to consume and be consumed by enchanting commodities. At the same time, the radical and religious right in America complain about moral turpitude in schools and believe that if we reintroduce a classical canon, prayer, and enforced virtue (plus police to search the students for weapons at each door of the school), the nation will be saved and our young will grow into good, solid citizens. It is not by chance that the right (always more knowledgeable than the left) spends so much time and energy on children, even the unborn, for they know that the Achilles' heel of the capitalist system can indeed be located in acculturation processes. Of course, there have been numerous critics from the left, such as Jonathan Kozol and Herbert Kohl,[10] and many educators who have developed programs to subvert the culture industry as best they can. Though negative artificiality may limit the effectiveness of such critiques and programs, they are still attacking the Achilles' heel of the system, in my estimation, and what may now seem artificial can take root and become more profound if the ground can be prepared for effective changes in the early education or socialization of children. Until much more of this preparation happens, we shall continue to witness mass processions celebrating the continual birth of lion kings presented as the future saviors of the realm.

6

Revisiting Benjamin's "The Storyteller"

Reviving the Past to Move Forward

There was once a young boy named Walter who wanted very much to make his life into a fairy tale, and it appeared at first that nothing could prevent him from realizing his wish. After all, he was born into a rich family, was smart, worked hard at school, and lived at a time when his country was prospering. However, Walter was marked. At first he did not feel the mark because his family's wealth protected him, and he could enjoy all the advantages and privileges of an upper-class life. This is not to say that Walter was spoiled. On the contrary, his parents set high standards and expected a great deal from him. And he did not deceive them but was himself deceived by the real conditions of his life.

When Walter began his studies at the university, he soon learned not only what the great philosophers had to say but also what his mark meant. He learned what it meant to be stigmatized, for he was told time and again that he was a Jew, that he was different, that he was not the same as the other people in his country. It was a great country, a country named Germany, a country that sought to make its mark on the world.

But Germany became too eager to exert its power, and it sought to make war with its neighbors. Nor were its neighbors disinclined to go to war. And so World War I began, and Walter was horrified.

He was a peace-loving person, a citizen of the world, who was against world wars, or wars of any kind. He protested the war, and he protested after the war. And he even thought of leaving his home country and going to Palestine to realize his dream of hope, his fairy-tale dream of the good society. But Walter had married and planned to teach at the university, for he was a bright philosopher, interested in imparting and sharing knowledge with the young, and it seemed that Germany had changed after the war. People were being treated more equally, even Jews like Walter. There was a lot of talk of socialism and communism that spelled hope for Walter. He met a young Russian woman, a gifted actress named Asja, who told him all about her work with children after the revolution in Russia and how she had developed new techniques of storytelling and dramatizing stories for children so that they could take charge of their lives. He wrote about her proletarian theater for children in the hope that the Germans would follow the example of the Russians. And he visited Asja in Russia, and he wrote about his experiences there. But back in Germany, he was still marked as a Jew and was prevented from teaching at the university. So Walter wrote books and worked for newspapers and the radio. He began associating with many thinkers and artists who wanted to change German society and make it more egalitarian and democratic. He now knew his individual fairy-tale dream could be realized only if life became a fairy tale for everyone. He placed great hope in children and began to create radio programs and stories for children. He broadcast these programs and tried to touch the imagination of thousands of young listeners with the voice of a storyteller. He had many plans for many programs, but his work for the radio station was abruptly canceled. Indeed, his entire life received an abrupt shock, for the Nazis had come to power, and he was now in danger and had to flee his country. The Nazis vowed to get rid of critical thinkers like Walter. They vowed to do away with Jews and other undesirables who might besmirch their alleged pure race.

Walter took refuge in a neighboring country, in France, and there he tried to work against the tyrants who had taken over his country. He reflected. He meditated. He spoke out. He wrote. He tried to understand what it was that had led his country to become so barbaric and violent. He wanted to save what was best in culture in order to save humanity. He wrote an essay about storytelling, about community, and the wise counsel of stories and storytellers. He wrote about technology and its power. He wrote about the necessity of sharing power and technology to benefit the lives of all people, not just the few, not just the rich, not just the Germans and Nazis. He wrote about the necessity for art to find new ways to reach out to people, to stimulate their thinking, and to provide deep pleasure.

But he had to stop writing and speaking out in Paris, for his life was again in danger. The Germans had invaded France and were marching toward Paris. So he packed his bags as fast as he could and traveled toward the Spanish border with a group of other people whose lives were also threatened by the fascists. Walter wanted to save himself. He wanted to save the fairy-tale hope that was still in him so he could continue to impart it to others. But he was also deceived and depressed. And when he came to the Spanish border and the Spanish police would not allow him and his friends to enter Spain, he imagined he would be turned over to the barbaric Nazis, and he was afraid, for he had heard many stories of beatings and torture.

So that night, the night that he was turned away from the Spanish border, Walter gave up the fairy tale and took some poison. When the Spanish police learned about his suicide, they had a change of heart and allowed the group of refugees to cross the border and escape the Nazis. Walter was buried in France—buried but not really dead.

This sad if not tragic story that I have just told is, of course, not a fairy tale. Yet, Walter Benjamin's life and works are filled with crucial fairy-tale elements that we must understand if we are to grasp why his short essay "The Storyteller" is worth revisiting. After his suicide in 1940 it appeared that his works would remain forgotten because the Nazis banned them. Even after the Nazis were defeated in 1945, Benjamin's works were not republished because there was no interest in critical theory during the 1950s and early 1960s.

There was a profound messianic element in everything he wrote, sparks of hope that glimmered like the hope in fairy tales. Therefore, it was not by chance that his critical essays were eventually rediscovered in the late 1960s, when the student revolutions in the West exploded and when other liberation movements around the world began gathering momentum. His hope for a more just and humane society was rekindled, and today his words have an almost magical power, a compelling urgency for all of us concerned with the dignity of humankind in the face of a new barbarism.

In particular, his essay "The Storyteller,"[1] written in 1936, is required reading for anyone who considers himself or herself a storyteller or cultural worker; anyone who wants to understand what storytelling was, can be, should be, might be, and is. But let me recapitulate the key ideas in this essay before I explain why I believe that it still has an urgent appeal and message for us today.

Benjamin subtitled his essay "Reflections on the Works of Nikolai Leskov," and he used Leskov, a remarkable but neglected nineteenth-century Russian writer, who incorporated in his writing all the best qualities of a storyteller as his model because he feared that the art of storytelling, oral and written, had undergone a demise, and Leskov provided an example and starting point for Benjamin to comment on storytelling in general. "Less and less one meets people who can truly tell stories. One encounters more and more frequently embarrassed faces among people when someone expresses the wish to hear a story. It is as though an ability that seemed to us to be inalienable, to be the most secure among secure things, had been taken from us. Namely, the ability to exchange experiences."[2]

Benjamin uses the German word *Erfahrung* for experience, not *Erlebnis*, another word that also means experience, and this careful use is important because Benjamin wants to make a distinction concerning the substance of what a storyteller relates and exchanges: *Erlebnis* is an event or happening that simply occurs without necessarily being fully comprehended, whereas *Erfahrung* denotes an experiential moment in which one learns something about oneself and the world. As Miriam Hansen points out, "*Erfahrung* does not have as much of an empiricist connotation as 'experience,' which links it to 'expert,' and 'experiment' and tends to assume a basically unmediated, stable relationship between subject and object. The German root of '*fahren*' (to ride, to travel), by contrast, conveys a sense of mobility, of journeying, wandering, or cruising, implying both a temporal dimension, that is, duration, habit, repetition, and return, and a degree of risk to the experiencing subject."[3] Thus, experience for Benjamin is a learning process through which one gains wisdom, and without the passing on of wisdom, there will be no genuine community or sharing.

Benjamin maintains that the archetypal storytellers were seafarers and farmers: The seafarers collected experiences on their voyages and in new and distant places; the farmers collected experiences at home, close to the earth, staying put, mining the soil. Of course there were other types of storytellers such as journeymen and spinners, but what Benjamin endeavors to establish is that true storytellers were craftspeople. Their stories were like their practical lives; they were handcrafted, sculpted, molded, hammered, forged, carved, sewn, or woven with ultimate care and savvy. The storytellers had a practical interest when they told their tales, and their stories were filled with counsel and wisdom. However, in 1936, when Benjamin was writing his essay, he argued that most people would find it old-fashioned if not archaic to talk about "knowing" or possessing wisdom. The reason, he states, is that "the communicability of experience has decreased. Consequently, we do not know how to give counsel to ourselves or to others. Counsel is indeed less an answer to a question than a proposal, the continuation of an ongoing story (that keeps rolling on). In order to obtain counsel, one must first of all be able to tell the story.... Counsel woven into the stuff of lived life is wisdom. The art of storytelling is moving toward its end because the narrative side of truth, which is wisdom, is perishing."[4]

Benjamin does not wax nostalgic about the decline of counsel, wisdom, and storytelling. When he says, "The secular historical forces of production ... have removed the story very gradually from the realm of living speech," he does not lament secularization because he believed that all kinds of religions conceal the truth of the real living conditions of people and that religious mythic

formations had to be pierced to free humans so that they could recognize who they were and what their power was. However, secularization did not mean the complete destruction of "mythic
religions." Rather, the new means of communication also preserved
what was beautiful in the mythic formations, which retained traces
of wisdom that could not be erased, for the beauty of wisdom was
independent of religion and myth and depended substantially on
the manner in which experience had been perceived and formu-
lated by the storyteller as indicative of something meaningful for
the community. Those stories of the ancient past, though related
to religions and myths that deceived, emanated from deeply felt
beliefs and experiences of groups of people that generated the need
for great storytellers who could counter the crude power of deceit
and hypocrisy through their art. Secularization had in part done
away with this need, but at the same time it had created the need
for a new kind of storytelling that would build upon the invaluable
art and work of past storytellers. Benjamin sought to grasp this need
and also to understand why there were so few great storytellers like
Leskov in his day. Therefore, his essay contains a short historical
analysis of how the printing press, the rise of the novel, and news
and stories in the mass media took precedence over storytelling, if
not eclipsed it. Everyone wants information and entertainment,
not wisdom, he argues. It is the *individual* private reading experience that counts. Nobody has the time to relax and listen, and the
art of listening has also declined. Nobody has a sense of history or
memory. Shared experience is not the basis of story anymore, and
genuine stories cannot be related if they do not come from the
experiences of the people.

   In opposition to this decline of storytellers and listeners, Benjamin, toward the end of his essay, projects his ideal of the great
storyteller to make his readers realize the "beauty" of what we may
lose forever. "A great storyteller will always be rooted in the
people,"[5] he claims, because he or she has the practical task of com-
municating wisdom as a use value to the people, and such mediation can effectively bring audiences closer to nature and endow
them with a sense of the possibilities for self-realization. Benjamin
especially praises the folk tale as the highest form of narrative:

"The folk tale, which to this day is the first tutor of children because it was once the first tutor of humankind, secretly lives on in the story. The first true storyteller is, and will continue to be, the teller of folk tales. Wherever good counsel was at a premium, the folk tale had it, and where the need was the greatest, its aid was nearest. This need was the need created by the myth. The folk tale tells us of the earliest arrangements that humankind made to shake off the nightmare which the myth had placed upon its chest.... The wisest thing—so the folk tale taught humankind in older times, and teaches children to this day—is to meet the forces of the mythical world with cunning and high spirits."[6]

It is interesting to read here that Benjamin opposes the folk tale to myth, which he associates with obfuscation, deception, and mystification. If we recall that Benjamin wrote his essay in 1936, when Hitler, Mussolini, and many other masterful orators were telling myths, when church leaders spoke mainly in the names of their institutions and not in the name of the people, we can see the political implications of his notion of the storyteller. For Benjamin, the storyteller carried light, that is enlightenment, to pierce the myths perpetuated by the dominant governmental, religious, and social institutions. Because these institutions legitimize themselves by fabricating mythic systems justifying and extolling their power, the genuine storyteller is by necessity subversive. Wisdom in a world of lies is subversive.

But what good did subversion do Benjamin? Why must great storytellers today be subversive? Why can't they celebrate their societies, their people, their customs? Wasn't Benjamin overly pessimistic about the decline of storytelling? After all, aren't we experiencing a renascence of storytelling throughout the world, despite horrendous ethnic conflicts? And weren't there genuine storytellers in his own time, perhaps storytellers whom he did not know? After all, Benjamin was a European thinker and knew very little about the oral traditions in Asia, Africa, South America, North America, and other parts of the world. Wasn't he, therefore, somewhat myopic? Or, given the Disneyization of the world, was he prophetic?

These are difficult questions, and if I were to try to answer them,

I would be compelled to develop an elaborate critique of Benjamin and point to some oversights and weaknesses in his essay. Though such a critique might be important, it is not my concern at the moment. I am more interested in reviving some of his more viable thoughts and moving forward with them, for I think his model of the "genuine" storyteller and his reflections about the demise of storytelling are pertinent for our own day and age, particularly if storytelling is going to play a role in preventing the kind of barbaric fascism that Benjamin experienced in his day. Indeed, storytelling is all around us, and unfortunately so are new and old kinds of barbarism. And if storytelling did not play an effective role in helping to undermine fascism in the 1930s, what can we expect of it today? What is its role today?

Indeed, storytelling is everywhere—in schools and libraries, in homes and in television tubes, in pubs and restaurants, during lunch breaks, in airports and train stations, on the phone, in theaters and cinemas. Contrary to what Benjamin believed, storytelling was not about to perish in the 1930s and certainly does not appear to be on the verge of perishing today. However, Benjamin was talking about a very particular kind of storytelling that does seem to be lost today—not completely, but it certainly seems to have been eclipsed by what I call commercialized, instrumentalized, or artificial storytelling.

Anyone can tell a good story. Anyone can perform and act out interesting stories: professionals and amateurs, young and old, male and female. Anyone can bill or sell himself or herself as a storyteller, but not everyone *is* a storyteller in Benjamin's sense of the term.

We live in societies that need stories for markets. Most stories, even those that originate from genuine experiences, are marketed for profit. Even the worst crimes and accidents are edited, cut, shaped, and disseminated by newscasters and telecasters as stories for a market of viewers. Every commercial that is projected on the television screen has a story to it. All of the newspapers and magazines print sensational stories to entice and titillate readers. Politicians are trained to tell stories to entertain audiences in the fashion of comedians. Comedians imitate politicians trying to act like comedians. Actors tell stories in films and about their lives. People commit atrocious crimes and sell their stories to publishers and television companies while in prison. Children hear and listen to all sorts of stories on television, on the radio, at home, and at school, and they act them out in play and in reality in their desire to become successful. Teachers tell stories to divert children, to quiet them down, to amuse them, to distract them.

For the most part, stories have become instrumentalized and commercialized in Western culture. Whether consciously or subconsciously, they are told for profit, to manipulate, to benefit someone's interests, and those interests are rarely those of a community or people. Whereas the work and customs of small tribes, towns, and communities shaped stories through the beginning of the nineteenth century, it is now the market, technology, and the routines of capitalist exchange that dictate how stories will be imparted and exchanged. The myth that Benjamin alluded to in "The Storyteller," the myth that needs contestation, is no longer the myth of Greco-Roman religion, feudalism, Christianity, or communism; it is much more nefarious. It is the myth of freedom in societies dominated by a capitalist market system that creates enormous barriers for the free exchange of ideas and experience. We think we speak freely in these societies. We think we are free to exchange our ideas. Yet our ideas are often prescripted, and our words are often petrified before we speak them.

Recall that Benjamin maintained that the ability or power to exchange experiences was at the heart of storytelling. He also argued that this inalienable ability or power seemed to have been taken from us. Exchange means that there must be a dialogue, a give and take, a sharing. As Peter Brooks has suggested, "Benjamin proposes ... the notion of narrative as gift: an act of generosity to which the receiver should respond by an equal generosity, either in telling another story (as in the model of the *Decameron* and its tradition), or in commenting on the story told, but in any event by the proof that the gift has been received, that the narrative has made a difference."[7] Exchange also means that there is not just one storyteller; the listener is also a storyteller, a receiver and giver of counsel, and counsel or wisdom is at the root of experience. A storyteller does not tell a story just for the sake of telling a story, to show off his or her own art, to simply amuse or divert. Even when a story is amusing, the storyteller never diverts but converts experience into hilarious wisdom, relates and infuses a comic anecdote with so much wisdom that it makes us burst with wise and knowing laughter. The storyteller is transformer, enlightener, and liberator. He or she takes personal experience and the experience of others and reflects upon that experience, digests it, relates it to the conditions of work and play in his or her society, and makes it part of his or her life before one word is uttered by his or her tongue. The storyteller can negate the commodity market by *exchanging experience* for counsel and wisdom.

Of course, there is a problem in our postmodern, postindustrial, totally computerized society that is dominated by the market. It is practically impossible to escape the market and conditions oriented to the market. If one wants to be a professional storyteller today, or even an amateur one, one must deal realistically with market conditions. One must continually face exploitation and oppression while trying to sell one's ability, talents, and power. It is difficult today to have a sense of community, a feeling of home and tradition.

Experience is alienation for most of us in Western societies. Paradoxically, we feel that we are alienated and cannot feel. We are no longer in touch with ourselves. We feel like automatons on a conveyer belt. We are born, bred, schooled, trained, given jobs, and fed amusements to regenerate ourselves so we can continue to work until we die. Our stories are transmitted to us through speaking voices on the radio, speaking and moving figures on movie and television screens, and words on computer screens. We think we recognize ourselves in the stories we hear and see. We think we know the stars of screen, television, and the tabloids. We think we belong to a gigantic family—to be sure, a dysfunctional family—some group, some community, some nation whose story unrolls before our eyes. If we don't belong, we want to belong. We crave identification and recognition. Each time we think we come close to recognizing who we are and what we can do with our immense talents and imagination, we are blocked because, as Benjamin suggests, we stumble against those market forces that make commodities out of our lives and create a new myth of freedom that actually conceals our daily alienating experiences.

This alienation is why the contemporary storyteller needs to know how to subvert artificial contrivances with artful stories based on experience, à la Benjamin. The storyteller must realize that he or she is *not* free to tell stories but has the power to liberate himself or herself and others through a genuine exchange of experience. The storyteller provokes thought and action through story, awakens the storyteller in others, listens, and seeks an opportunity to tell another story that subverts the myth of freedom. The storyteller knows he or she is free to subvert. It is this knowledge, this experience, that must be exchanged today as we move toward recreating the role of the storyteller.

However, let there be no mistake about Benjamin's attitude toward the situation of the storyteller in our advanced computerized capitalist society. As he made clear in another famous essay, "The Work of Art in the Age of Mechanical Reproduction," Benjamin was against not the latest technological inventions but the manner in which they might be used to entrance, captivate, and deceive people. For instance, he felt that the cinema was extremely important because it enabled more people to see the reproduction of images that could be shared, enjoyed, and discussed for their own pleasure and enlightenment, but only as long as they had some control over what was to be produced and reproduced. He argued in 1936, when fascism was growing stronger, that there was an aestheticization of politics that was most dangerous because the beautiful spectacle—myths, mass rallies, parades—was being used to cover up the dirty conditions of politics, namely, Nazism. He felt that we were at a turning point in the 1930s and that the technological means of reproduction, which could be so democratic and liberating, had to be accessible to the people so that they could represent or exchange their experiences. He never gave up hope that the radio and cinema—he did not live long enough to become acquainted with television—might be utilized to exchange experiences in the manner of the authentic storytellers of the past.

Some critical theorists who were close to Benjamin, such as Theodor Adorno and Max Horkheimer, who wrote about the overwhelming power of the culture industry in *Dialectic of Enlighten-ment*, and Herbert Marcuse, who developed pessimistic ideas of conformity in *One-Dimensional Man*, thought that it was almost impossible to combat the aestheticization of politics and convert the means of production to give more democratic expression to the voice of the people, but I think that Benjamin himself, if he were alive today, would not have shared their position. In fact, I believe that he would have looked for gaps and traces of hope in the cul-ture industry and one-dimensional societies that might enable peo-ple to distribute and share their experiences to undermine conformity. And indeed, there are some signs of hope in television with such productions as *Sesame Street* or Jim Henson's provocative *The Storyteller*, a unique series of folk tales that not only incorpo-rated a questioning attitude toward storytelling but also cultivated a sense of sharing wisdom with the audience. In the film industry, a film like *Into the West* is a model; it depicts how Irish legend and myth can empower two young boys who are oppressed by a corrupt bureaucracy and alienated from their father and community. Even more fascinating than film and television is the manner in which millions of people are using the Internet to share experiences, information, and knowledge. A new kind of public space (which has become threatened by government control and private indus-try) has opened up in which people engage one another to discuss, debate, tell stories, and communicate news. The purpose of the narrators recalls that of storytellers within a community except that here the community is always in the process of being created, keeps shifting, and demands that we shift and open ourselves up to new ways of thinking. Our allegiances are not bound to one particular group or class. Choice and tolerance are fostered. The verbal exchanges lead to reflection and wisdom.

Of course, one could point to the example of Salman Rushdie as an example of a writer and storyteller who fosters such reflection in many ways. He has reflected upon his own situation in *Haroun and the Sea of Stories* (1990) and used the mass media and culture indus-try to make his voice heard. Sentenced to death in 1988 by the Ayatollah Khomeini,[8] Rushdie wrote *Haroun and the Sea of Stories* ostensibly for his son, and it begins:

Z *embla, Zenda Xanadu*
A *ll our dream-worlds may come true.*
F *airy lands are fearsome too.*
A *s I wander far from view*
R *ead, and bring me home to you.*[9]

This dedication is a call not just to his son but to all of us to bring back the storyteller and truthful storytelling to the world in the manner that Benjamin described it. Rushdie's novel, which has many interpretative levels, concerns Rashid, the shah of Blah, who is blessed with the gift of gab. He shares this gift with the people of his country, but one day he is unable to tell tales, for his power is mysteriously controlled by Khattam-Shud, who, as Rashid explains to his son Haroun, is "the Arch-Enemy of all Stories, even of Language itself. He is the Prince of Silence and the Foe of Speech. And because everything ends, because dreams end, stories end, life ends, at the finish of everything we use his name. 'It's finished,' we tell one another, 'it's over. Khattam-Shud: The End.'"[10] But it is not the end in the novel. Rather, it is the beginning for Haroun, who eventually defeats Khattam-Shud so that his father regains his talent and can once again tell stories. Unfortunately, in reality the forces of silence have not been completely defeated because Rushdie must still live in hiding and must fear for his life. However, he continues to write; issue statements; make public appearances; and speak out for storytelling that exposes the abuse of power, hypocrisy, and superstition. He tells about his own situation, and in his telling, whether written or oral, he creates criteria of "genuine" storytelling that encourage readers to find and maintain their own voices and sea of stories.

These examples are just a few illustrations of how storytellers enter the culture industry to "subvert" it, or at the very least to question and challenge its machinations. They suggest the recreation of the storyteller as wise provocateur, and of course there are other more direct means that storytellers use within the oral tradition, that is, face to face with audiences, that provide listeners with counsel about how to overcome alienation and allow for an exchange of experience. There are storytellers who use every means possible to empower listeners to realize their own talents as storytellers and to keep alive a sense of community. There are storytellers who are first and foremost listeners, who listen to the crises and struggles in our societies and try through listening to the temper of our times to extrapolate wisdom and hope in creative ways. Whatever choice the storyteller makes today in light of massive social and technological changes, I believe that it is crucial to keep Benjamin's ideal storyteller in mind. Perhaps, given the barbarism and the conflicts over freedom throughout the world, his ideal cannot be realized right now. But there certainly is something indelible about it, something utopian that is worth contemplating and worth pursuing as we move forward to tell our next story.

Notes

Introduction

1. David Denby, "Buried Alive: Our Children and the Avalanche of Crud," *New Yorker* 72 (July 15, 1996): 51.
2. Hermann Bausinger, *Folk Culture in a World of Technology*, trans. Elke Dettmer (Bloomington: Indiana University Press, 1990): 152.
3. Ibid., 153.

Chapter 1

1. For one of the more comprehensive collections of cat tales that deal with a variety of themes, see John Richard Stephens, ed., *The King of the Cats and Other Feline Fairy Tales* (London: Faber and Faber, 1993).
2. See also Patricia Dale-Green, *Cult of the Cat* (Boston: Houghton Mifflin, 1963); Mildred Kirk, *The Everlasting Cat* (Woodstock, NY: Overland Press, 1985); and John Richard Stephens, *The Enchanted Cat* (Rocklin, Calif.: Prima Publishing and Communications, 1990).
3. Marina Warner, *From the Beast to the Blonde: On Fairytales and Their Tellers* (London: Chatto and Windus, 1994). Warner argues that the power of storytelling was either wrested from

the hands of women or that their storytelling was denigrated by being likened to silly gossip or prattle. Whatever the case may be, the literary tradition is marked by male dominance.

4. See *The Facetious Nights of Straparola*, trans. W. G. Waters, illustr. Jules Garnier and E. R. Hughes, 4 vols. (London: Society of Bibliophiles, 1894). In the fourth volume is an excellent "Terminal Essay" (237–74) by Waters that provides the literary and social background to Straparola's work.

5. Giambattista Basile, *Lo Cunto de li Cunti*, ed. Michele Rak (Milan: Garzanti, 1986): 332–33, my translation. Rak's edition is excellent because it contains Basile's original dialect version with Rak's translation into standard Italian on facing pages. For another excellent translation of the Neapolitan text into standard Italian, see Giambattista Basile, *Il racconto dei racconti*, ed. Alessandra Burani and Ruggero Guarini, trans. Ruggero Guarini (Milan: Adelphi Edizioni, 1994).

6. Basile, *Lo Cunto de li Cunti*, 332–33, my translation.

7. Basile, *Lo Cunto de li Cunti*, 12–13, my translation.

8. Barbara Broggini, *"Lo cunto de li cunti" von Giambattista Basile: Ein Ständepoet in Streit mit der Plebs, Fortuna und der höfischen Korruption* (Frankfurt am Main: Peter Lang, 1990): 95–102.

9. See Denise Escarpit, *Histoire d'un conte: Le Chat Botté en France et en Angleterre*, vol. 1 (Paris: Didier, 1985): 88–120.

10. Jack Zipes, ed., *Beauties, Beasts, and Enchantment: Classic French Fairy Tales* (New York: New American Library, 1989): 21.

11. Ibid., p. 24.

12. Louis Marin, "*Puss-in-Boots*: Power of Signs—Signs of Power," *Diacritics* 7 (June 1977): 57.

13. Philip Lewis, *Seeing Through the Mother Goose Tales: Visual Turns in the Writings of Charles Perrault* (Stanford: Stanford University Press, 1996).

14. Ibid., 40–41.

15. Ibid., 148.

16. Ibid., 148.

17. See "Puss in Boots" in Jacob and Wilhelm Grimm, *The Complete Fairy Tales of the Brothers Grimm*, ed. and trans. Jack Zipes (New York: Bantam, 1987): 652–55.

18. For a comprehensive study of Disney's early films, see Russsell Merritt and J. B. Kaufman, *Walt in Wonderland: The Silent Films of Walt Disney* (Baltimore: Johns Hopkins University Press, 1993):14.

Chapter 2

1. Regina Böhm-Korff, *Deutung und Bedeutung von "Hänsel and Gretel": Eine Fallstudie* (Frankfurt am Main: Peter Lang, 1991). There is also another book in German by Ursula Eschenbach, *Hänsel und Gretel: Das geheime Wissen der Kinder* (Stuttgart: Kreuz Verlag, 1986), but I find this pseudo-Jungian self-help book filled with simplistic and misleading interpretations that are framed within a fictitious and melodramatic narrative. Much more rewarding is Jacqueline Schectman's Jungian analysis in her chapter "'Hansel and Gretel' and the Impoverished Stepmother" in *The Stepmother in Fairy Tales: Bereavement and the Feminine Shadow* (Boston: Sigo Press, 1993): 51–78. By trying to understand the stepmother's psyche and social condition, Schectman sheds new light on the tale.

2. See Heinz Rölleke, ed., *Die älteste Märchensammlung der Brüder Grimm* (Cologne-Genève: Fondation Martin Bodmer, 1975). Between 1807 and 1810, the Grimms began collecting tales with the express purpose of sending them to their friend Clemens Brentano, the famous poet, who intended to publish a collection of traditional folk tales. Since they were worried that the unreliable Brentano might take great liberties with the stories, they had copies made of the forty-six texts that they sent to him. Ironically, he never made use of them but abandoned them in the Ölenberg Monastery in Alsace, while the Grimms destroyed their copies of the precious manuscripts after they themselves had changed them for their first edition. Only in 1920 were the handwritten tales rediscovered, and they were published in different editions in 1924, 1927, and 1975. The most recent publication, edited by Rölleke, is the most scholarly and useful, for he has carefully shown how the Grimms' original handwritten manuscripts can help us document their sources and reveal the great changes the brothers made in shaping the tales.

3. See August Stöber, *Volksbüchlein: Kinder- und Volksliedchen, Spielreime, Sprüche und Märchen* (Strasburg: G. L. Schuler, 1842): 102–109.

4. Rölleke, *Die älteste Märchen Sammlung der Brüder Grimm*, 70.

5. Ibid., 76.

6. *The Complete Fairy Tales of the Brothers Grimm*, ed. and trans. Jack Zipes (New York: Bantam, 1987): 58.

7. Ibid., 63–64.

8. Ibid., 62.

9. Ibid., 63.

10. Ibid., 64.

11. See Rüdiger Steinlein, *Die domestizierte Phantasie: Studien zur Kinderliteratur, Kinderlektüre und Literaturpädagogk des 18. Jahrhunderts und frühen 19. Jahrhunderts.* (Heidelberg: Carl Winter Universitätsverlag, 1987).

12. Rüdiger Steinlein, *Märchen als poetische Erziehungsform: Zum kinderliterarischen Status der Grimmschen "Kinder- und Hausmärchen,"* Heft 29 (Berlin: Humboldt-Universität, 1994).

13. Shulamith Shahar, *Childhood in the Middle Ages* (London: Routledge, 1990): 116.

14. See Engelbert Humperdinck and Adelheid Wette, *Hänsel und Gretel*, ed. Wolfram Humperdinck (Stuttgart: Reclam, 1952).

15. Ibid., 46–47, my translation. I have rendered the poetry into literal prose.

16. See Alice Miller, *The Drama of the Gifted Child*, trans. Ruth Ward (New York: Basic Books, 1981) and *For Your Own Good: Hidden Cruelty in Child-Rearing and the Roots of Violence* (New York: Basic Books, 1983).

17. John Boswell, *The Kindness of Strangers: The Abandonment of Children in Western Europe from Late Antiquity to the Renaissance* (New York: Pantheon, 1988): 99.

18. Ibid., 122.

19. Ibid., p. 123.

Chapter 3

1. Rudolph Schenda, *Von Mund zu Ohr: Bausteine zu einer Kulturgeschichte volkstümlichen Erzählens in Europa* (Göttingen:

Vandenhoeck and Ruprecht, 1993). Schenda questions whether nonliterate people were as capable in telling fairy tales and other complex narratives as we seem to think they were, and he questions general assumptions about the widespread role and function of storytelling in Europe in relation to the rise of literacy.

2. Gerald Mast, *A Short History of the Movies* (New York: Pegasus, 1971): 45.

3. Donald Crafton, *Before Mickey: The Animated Film, 1898–1928* (Cambridge, Mass.: MIT Press, 1982): 11.

4. See Russell Merritt and J. B. Kaufman, *Walt in Wonderland: The Silent Films of Walt Disney* (Baltimore: Johns Hopkins University Press, 1993).

5. When Disney built his Burbank studio in 1939, he took pride in the fact that he could provide a special lounge for his male workers to gather without female intervention. In *Walt Disney: Hollywood's Dark Prince* (New York: Birch Lane Press, 1993), Marc Eliot comments: "Disney took great pleasure in a studio press release describing the club as a 'womanless paradise for the recreational use of the Disney male employees. The women may have taken over the bars and the barber shops, but they still can't crash the profession of animation. The only skirted artists in the studio are the girls who trace the animators' drawings onto celluloid and paint them'" (108–109). Several critics have drawn attention to the phallic jokes in Disney's films, but to my knowledge, there has not been a serious study of the male infantile humor in the Disney cinematic productions. In *Pinocchio*, we can see it at work when Jiminy Cricket accidentally places his arm on the rear end of a female porcelain figure and when he gapes at the can-can marionettes in Stromboli's theater.

6. See Richard Wunderlich, *The Pinocchio Catalogue* (New York: Greenwood, 1988), for the most exhaustive list of texts.

7. Carlo Collodi, *The Adventures of Pinocchio*, trans. and intro. Nicolas J. Perella (Berkeley: University of California Press, 1986): 82.

8. Ibid., 131.

9. Ibid., 135.

10. For two interesting biographies of Disney, see Leonard Mosley, *Disney's World* (New York: Stein and Day, 1985), and Marc Eliot, *Walt Disney: Hollywood's Dark Prince* (New York: Birch Lane Press, 1993).

11. See Merritt and Kaufman, *Walt in Wonderland*.

12. See Mosley, *Disney's World*, 177: "This would be a break-through film for all of them, he said, in which all the lessons and new techniques they had learned from *Snow White* would be implemented and perfected, and all the mistakes they had made in earlier films would be rectified. 'What I will be looking for in this production will be color and dimension and wonderful effects of a kind that has never been seen in animated movies before,' he said. 'It will be the costliest cartoon film ever made, but we've got the money in the bank (which was true at the moment)—and damn the expense. Because *Pinocchio* is going to be the biggest challenge in the history of animation.'"

13. Richard Wunderlich and Thomas J. Morrissey. "The Dese-cration of *Pinocchio* in the United States," *The Horn Book Magazine* 58 (April 1982): 211.

14. Richard Schickel, *The Disney Version: The Life, Times, Art and Commerce of Walt Disney* (New York: Simon and Schuster, 1968): 232–33.

15. The supervising directors were Ben Sharpsteen and Hamilton Luske; sequence directors Bill Roberts, Norman Ferguson, Jack Kinney, Wilfred Jackson, and T. Hee; animation directors Fred Moore, Franklin Thomas, Milton Kahl, Vladimir Tytla, Ward Kimball, Arthur Babbitt, Eric Larson, and Wolfgang Reithmann; story adaptation Ted Sears, Otto Englander, Webb Smith, William Cottrell, Joseph Sabo, Erdman Penner, and Aurelius Battaglia; music and lyrics Leigh Harline, Ned Washington, and Paul J. Smith. For further information, see Leonard Maltin, *The Disney Films*, updated edition (New York: Crown, 1984): 32–37.

16. See Douglas Street, "*Pinocchio*: From Picaro to Pipsqueak," in *Children's Novels and the Movies*, ed. Douglas Street (New York: Frederick Ungar, 1983): 47–57.

Chapter 4

1. Eric Loren Smoodin, *Animating Culture: Hollywood Cartoons from the Sound Era* (New Brunswick: Rutgers University Press, 1993): 188.

2. Richard de Cordova, "The Mickey in Macy's Window: Childhood, Consumerism, and Disney Animation," in *Disney Discourse: Producing the Magic Kingdom*, ed. Eric Loren Smoodin (New York: Routledge, 1994): 204.

3. "The Big Bad Wolf," *Fortune* 10 (November 1934): 88.

4. Richard Schickel, *The Disney Version: The Life, Times, Art and Commerce of Walt Disney* (New York: Simon and Schuster, 1968): 206.

5. See Donald Crafton, *Before Mickey: The Animated Film, 1898–1928* (Cambridge, Mass.: MIT Press, 1982): 1–33. With regard to Disney, Crafton states, "Perhaps the aspect that most set Disney's series apart from his competitors' was the overtly libidinous (but presumably naive) content of the humor. Present audiences cannot help but be impressed by the extent to which phallic imagery informs the majority of gags ..." (294).

6. See Andrea Rothman, "The Henson Kids Carry On," *Business Weekly* 3198 (February 4, 1991): 72–73. Before he died, Henson was negotiating a $150 million deal for the Disney Studios to purchase Henson Productions. The sale was eventually blocked by Michael Eisner of Disney for undisclosed reasons, and in my opinion, its failure may be a blessing in disguise for Henson Productions.

7. Jerry Juhl wrote the screenplay. The princess was played by Trudy Young, the prince by Gordon Thomson. The film was coproduced by Henson Associates and VTR Productions (Canada).

8. This ending may also be a hidden reference to the well-known lines in *Annie Hall* by Woody Allen: "You know, even as a kid I always went for the wrong women. When my mother took me to see *Snow White*, everyone fell in love with Snow White; I immediately fell for the Wicked Queen."

9. See the book based on the television series, Anthony

Minghella, *Jim Henson's "The Storyteller,"* illustr. Darcy May (New York: Knopf, 1991).

10. "Miss Piggy Went to Market and $150 Million Came Home," an interview with Jim Henson, *American Film* 15 (November 1989): 20.

11. "The Shelley and Ted Show," *Forbes*, February 5, 1990: 174.

12. Tom Davenport, "Making Grimm Movies," *From the Brothers Grimm* 5 (1993): 1. See also Tom Davenport, "Some Personal Notes on Adapting Folk-Fairy Tales to Film," *Children's Literature* 9 (1981): 107–115.

13. See Anthony L. Manna, "The Americanization of the Brothers Grimm, or Tom Davenport's Film Adaptations of German Folktales," *Children's Literature Quarterly* 13 (Fall 1988): 142–54.

14. The newsletter is called *From the Brothers Grimm* and is published by Davenport Films in Delaplane, Virginia. Each issue generally focuses on one of Davenport's films. For instance, vol. 3, issue 1 of 1990 featured a discussion of "Cinderella" and "Ashpet."

15. At present, Davenport is at work adapting *Snow White* for the screen. He has taken a Kentucky folk tale, "The Step Child That Was Treated Mighty Bad," collected by Marie Campbell, and has set the story in the South during the 1920s. His treatment of the rivalry between the stepmother and stepdaughter takes an unusual twist. The stepmother is a former actress who has seen her better days in the theater. When her stepdaughter runs away and begins performing with a traveling medicine man who also does a sideshow, the young girl's talents blossom. She is discovered by a young filmmaker, her "prince," who wants to help her make a career in movies. By altering and transforming the plot, Davenport also comments on the "rivalry" between the theater and cinema, that is, on the rise of cinema in the 1920s.

16. There are also numerous fairy-tale films that continue to reflect the standardized mediocrity of the Disney productions and ideology. For instance, The Cannon Group produced a series of films in 1987–1988, *The Emperor's New Clothes, Hansel and*

Gretel, Rumpelstiltskin, Sleeping Beauty, Snow White, and *Red Riding Hood,* which had dubious value. Operating with stars (Amy Irving, Sid Caesar, Diana Rigg, and Isabella Rossellini among others) as Shelley Duvall did, the executive producers Menahmen Golan and Yoram Globus, accomplished something surprising by making fairy tales look stale on the screen. A reviewer for *Variety* commented, "Will Cannon's Movie-tales sell tickets? Maybe, but only if the kiddies and their parents want to watch thoroughly unsophisticated but very straightforward storytelling with only the slightest inkling of modern technical production values" (May 27, 1987: 16). More recently, in 1994, HBO produced a series of multicultural animated fairy-tale films entitled *Happily Ever After Fairy Tales for Every Child*. Once again, the classics were thoughtlessly reproduced, and the only change is an "ethnic twist" that makes it seem as if HBO and Random House have the welfare of children in mind. However, the only thing these corporations have in mind is selling coloring books, stickers, place mats, and activity kits that one can order when one buys the videocassette of a particular tale.

17. *The Fractured Fairy Tales* were narrated by Edward Everett Horton and were part of the American television series *Rocky and His Friends* and *The Bullwinkle Show*. This series is currently being reproduced for the American cable television channel Nickleodeon as *The Adventures of Rocky and Bullwinkle*.

Chapter 5

1. Theodor Adorno, *The Culture Industry*, ed. J. M. Bernstein (London: Routledge, 1991): 33–34.
2. Ibid., 34.
3. Ibid., 35.
4. David Denby, "Buried Alive: Our Children and the Avalanche of Crud," *The New Yorker* 72 (July 15, 1996): 52.
5. Marsha Kinder, *Playing with Power in Movies, Television, and Video Games: From Muppet Babies to Teenage Mutant Ninja Turtles* (Berkeley: University of California Press, 1991).
6. See Paul Piccone, "The Changing Function of Critical Theory,"

New German Critique 12 (Fall 1977): 29–38; "Labriola and the Roots of Eurocommunism," *Berkeley Journal of Sociology* 22 (1977–1978): 3–44; and "The Crisis of One-Dimensionality," *Telos* (1978): 48.

7. Piccone, "The Crisis of One-Dimensionality," 48.
8. Ibid., 51–52.
9. Bernstein's introduction to Adorno, *The Culture Industry*, 21–22.
10. See Jonathan Kozol, *Savage Inequalities* (New York: HarperCollins, 1991), and Herbert Kohl, *"I Won't Learn From You and Others": Thoughts on Creative Maladjustment* (New York: New Press, 1994).

Chapter 6

1. Walter Benjamin, "The Storyteller: Reflections on the Works of Nikolai Leskov," *Illuminations*, trans. Harry Zohn (New York: Harcourt, Brace and World, 1968): 83–109.
2. Ibid., 83. I have altered the translation.
3. Miriam Hansen, "Foreword," in Oskar Negt and Alexander Kluge, *Public Sphere and Experience: Toward an Analysis of the Bourgeois and Proletarian Public Sphere*, trans. Peter Labanyi, Jamie Owen Daniel, and Asskenka Oksiloff (Minneapolis: University of Minnesota Press, 1993): xvi–xvii.
4. Benjamin, "The Storyteller," 86–87. I have altered the translation.
5. Ibid., 101.
6. Ibid., 102. I have altered the translation.
7. Peter Brooks, *Psychoanalysis and Storytelling* (London: Blackwell, 1994): 87.
8. For background information, see W. J. Weatherby, *Salman Rushdie: Sentenced to Death* (New York: Carroll and Graf, 1990).
9. Salman Rushdie, *Haroun and the Sea of Stories* (New York: Viking, 1990): 11.
10. Ibid., 39.

Bibliography

Adorno, Theodor. *The Culture Industry*. Ed. J. M. Bernstein. London: Routledge, 1991.

Bacon, Martha. "Puppet's Progress: Pinocchio." In *Children and Literature: Views and Reviews*, ed. Virginia Havilland. Glenview, Ill.: Scott, Foresman, 1973. 71–77.

Bakhtin, M.M. *Speech Genres and Other Late Essays*. Eds. Caryl Emerson and Michael Holquist. Trans. Vernon W. McGee. Austin: University of Texas, 1986.

Barberi Squarotti, G. "Problemi di technica narrativa cinquecentesca." *Sigma* 2 (1965), 84–108.

Basile, Giambattista. *The Pentamerone of Giambattista Basile*. Trans. and ed. N. M. Penzer. 2 vols. London: John Lane the Bodley Head, 1932.

———. *Lo Cunto de li Cunti*. Ed. Michele Rak. Milan: Garazanti, 1986.

———. *Il racconto dei racconti*. Ed. Alessandra Burani and Ruggero Guarini. Trans. Ruggero Guarini. Milan: Adelphi Edizioni, 1994.

Bausinger, Hermann. *Folk Culture in a World of Technology*. Trans. Elke Dettmer. Bloomington: Indiana University Press, 1990.

Bell, Elizabeth, Lynda Haas, and Laura Sells, eds. *From Mouse to*

Mermaid: The Politics of Film, Gender, and Culture. Blooming-ton: Indiana University Press, 1995.

Benjamin, Jessica. *The Bonds of Love: Psychoanalysis, Feminism, and the Problem of Domination*. New York: Pantheon, 1988.

Benjamin, Walter. *Illuminations*. Trans. Harry Zohn. New York: Harcourt, Brace & World, 1968.

Birch, Carol L., and Melissa A. Heckler, eds. *Who Says? Essays on Pivotal Issues in Contemporary Storytelling*. Little Rock:, Ark.: August House, 1996.

Bly, Robert. *Iron John: A Book about Men*. Reading, Mass.: Addi-son-Wesley, 1990.

Böhm-Korff, Regina. *Deutung und Bedeutung von "Hänsel und Gretel": Eine Fallstudie*. Frankfurt am Main: Peter Lang, 1991.

Boswell, John. *The Kindness of Strangers: The Abandonment of Children in Western Europe from Late Antiquity to the Renaissance*. New York: Pantheon, 1988.

Briggs, Katharine M. *Nine Lives: The Folklore of Cats*. New York: Pantheon, 1980.

Broggini, Barbara. *"Lo cunto de li Cunti" von Giambattista Basile: Ein Ständepoet in Streit mit der Plebs, Fortuno und der höfischen Korruption*. Frankfurt am Main: Peter Lang, 1990.

Brooks, Peter. *Psychoanalysis and Storytelling*. London: Blackwell, 1994.

Burke, Peter. *The Italian Renaissance: Culture and Society in Italy*. Rev. ed. Princeton: Princeton University Press, 1987.

Cambi, Franco. *Collodi, De Amicis, Rodari: Tre immagini d'infanzia*. Bari: Edizioni Dedalo, 1985.

Cambon, Glauco. "Pinocchio and the Problem of Children's Lit-erature." *Children's Literature* 2 (1973): 50–60.

Card, Claudia. "Pinocchio." In *From Mouse to Mermaid: The Poli-tics of Film, Gender, and Culture*. Eds. Elizabeth Bell, Lynda Haas, and Laura Sells. Bloomington: Indiana University Press, 1995. 62–71.

"Carlo Collodi." *Children's Literature Review*. Ed. Gerald J. Senick. Detroit: Gale Research, 1983. 69–87.

Caro, Frank de, ed. *The Folktale Cat*. Illustr. Kitty Harvill. Little Rock, Ark.: August House, 1992.

Caron-Lowins, Evelyne. "Il Était mille fois, il sera encore ..." *La Revue du Cinema* 401 (1985): 43–48.

Cholodenko, Alan, ed. *The Illusion of Life: Essays on Animation.* Sydney: Power Publications in Association with the Australian Film Commission, 1991.

Collodi, Carlo. *The Adventures of Pinocchio.* Trans. and intro. Nicolas J. Perella. Berkeley: University of California Press, 1986.

Crafton, Donald. *Before Mickey: The Animated Film, 1898–1928.* Cambridge, Mass.: MIT Press, 1982.

Cro, Stelio. "When Children's Literature Becomes Adult." *Merveilles et Contes* 7 (1993): 87–112.

Dale-Green, Patricia. *Cult of the Cat.* Boston: Houghton Mifflin, 1963.

Datlow, Ellen, and Terri Windling, eds. *Black Thorn, White Rose.* New York: William Morrow, 1993.

———, eds. *Snow White, Blood Red.* New York: William Morrow, 1994.

———, eds. *Ruby Slippers, Golden Tears.* New York: William Morrow, 1995.

Davenport, Tom. "Some Personal Notes on Adapting Folk-Fairy Tales to Film." *Children's Literature* 9 (1981): 107–115.

———. "Making Grimm Movies." *From the Brothers Grimm* 5 (1993): 1, 6–7.

Davenport, Tom, and Gary Carden. *From the Brothers Grimm: A Contemporary Retelling of American Folktales and Classic Stories.* Fort Atkinson, Wis.: Highsmith Press, 1992.

Denby, David. "Buried Alive: Our Children and the Avalanche of Crud." *The New Yorker* 72 (July 15, 1996): 48–58.

Eliot, Marc. *Walt Disney: Hollywood's Dark Prince.* New York: Birch Lane Press, 1993.

Escarpit, Denise. *Histoire d'un conte: Le Chat Botté en France et en Angleterre.* 2 vols. Paris: Didier, 1985.

Eschenbach, Ursula. *Hänsel und Gretel: Das geheime Wissen der Kinder.* Stuttgart: Kreuz Verlag, 1986.

Estés, Clarissa Pinkola. *Women Who Run with the Wolves: Myths and Stories of the Wild Woman Archetype.* New York: Ballantine, 1993.

Fanning, Deidre. "The Shelley and Ted Show." *Forbes* 145 (February 5, 1990): 172–74.

Fiske, John. *Understanding Popular Culture*. London: Unwin Hyman, 1989.

Gannon, Susan R. "A Note on Collodi and Lucian." *Children's Literature* 8 (1980): 98–192.

———. "*Pinocchio*: The First Hundred Years." *Children's Literature Association Quarterly* 6 (Winter 1981–1982): 1 ff.

Garner, James Finn. *Politically Correct Bedtime Stories*. New York: Macmillan, 1994.

———. *Once Upon a More Enlightened Time: More Politically Correct Fairy Tales*. New York: Macmillan, 1995.

———. *Politically Correct Holiday Stories: For an Enlightened Yuletide Season*. New York: Macmillan, 1996.

Gingold, Alfred. *Fire in the John: The Manly Man in the Age of Sissification*. New York: St. Martin's Press, 1991.

Goforth, Frances S., and Carolyn V. Spilman. *Using Folk Literature in the Classroom: Encouraging Children to Read and Write*. Phoenix: Oryx Press, 1994.

Graham, Barbara. *Women Who Run with the Poodles: Myths and Tips for Honoring Your Mood Swings*. New York: Avon, 1994.

Grimm, Brüder. *Kinder- und Hausmärchen*. Ed. Heinz Rölleke. 3 vols. Stuttgart: Reclam, 1980.

Grimm, Jacob and Wilhelm. *The Complete Fairy Tales of the Brothers Grimm*. Ed. and trans. Jack Zipes. New York: Bantam, 1987.

Hansen, Miriam. "Foreword." In Oskar Negt and Alexander Kluge. *Public Sphere and Experience: Toward an Analysis of the Bourgeois and Proletarian Public Sphere*. Trans. Peter Labanyi, Jamie Owen Daniel, and Asskenka Oksiloff. Minneapolis: University of Minnesota Press, 1993.

Heins, Paul. "A Second Look: *The Adventures of Pinocchio*." *Horn Book Magazine* 58 (1982): 200–204.

Heisig, James W. "Pinocchio: Archetype of the Motherless Child." *Children's Literature* 3 (1974): 23–35.

Horkheimer, Max, and Theodor W. Adorno. *Dialectic of Enlightenment*. Trans. John Cumming. New York: Seabury Press, 1972.

"How to Help Your Kids Get the Most from TV." *TV Guide* 39 (March 2–8, 1991): 5–9.

Humperdinck, Engelbert, and Adelheid Wette. *Hänsel and Gretel.* Ed. Wolfram Humperdinck. Stuttgart: Reclam, 1952.

Hutchings, David. "Enchantress Shelley Duvall Creates a Magic Garden in Her Faerie Tale Theatre for TV." *People Weekly* 20 (September 12, 1983): 58–60.

Irmen, Hans-Josef. *Hänsel und Gretel: Studien und Dokumente zu Engelbert Humperdincks Märchenoper.* Mainz: Schott, 1989.

Jacoby, Mario, Verena Kast, and Ingrid Reidel. *Witches, Ogres, and the Devil's Daughter: Encounters with Evil in Fairy Tales.* Trans. Michael H. Kohn. Boston: Shambhala, 1992.

Kantrowitz, Barbara. "Fractured Fairy Tales." *Newsweek* 112 (July 18, 1988): 64.

Kirk, Mildred. *The Everlasting Cat.* Woodstock, N.Y.: Overlook Press, 1985.

Knowles, Murray, and Kirsten Malmkjaer. *Language and Control in Children's Literature.* London: Routledge, 1996.

Larvaille, Pierre. *Perspectives et limites d'une analyse morphologique due conte, pour une révision du schéma de Propp.* Paris: Centre de recherches de langue et littérature italienne, Université Paris X-Nanterre, 1973.

Leach, Penelope. *Children First.* New York: Knopf, 1994.

Lenburg, Jeff. *The Encyclopedia of Animated Cartoons.* New York: Facts on File, 1991.

Lewis, Philip. *Seeing Through the Mother Goose Tales: Visual Turns in the Writings of Charles Perrault.* Stanford: Stanford University Press, 1996.

Loevy, Diana. "Inside the House That Henson Built." *Channels* 8 (March 1988): 52–53.

Lulow, Kalia. "Fractured Fairy Tales." *Connoisseur* 214 (November 1984): 54–55.

Magid, Ron. "*Labyrinth* and *Legend*, Big Screen Fairy Tales." *American Cinematographer* 67 (August 1986): 65–70.

Maltin, Leonard. *The Disney Films.* Updated edition. New York: Crown, 1984.

Manna, Anthony L. "The Americanization of the Brothers

Grimm, or Tom Davenport's Film Adaptations of German Folktales." *Children's Literature Quarterly* 13 (Fall 1988): 142–54.

Marcuse, Herbert. *One-Dimensional Man: Studies in the Ideology of Advanced Industrial Society*. Boston: Beacon, 1964.

Marin, Louis. "*Puss-in-Boots:* Power of Signs—Signs of Power." *Diacritics* 7 (June 1977): 54–63.

Martines, Lauro. *An Italian Renaissance Sextet: Six Tales in Historical Context*. Trans. Murtha Baca. New York: Marsilio, 1994.

Mast, Gerald. *A Short History of the Movies*. New York: Pegasus, 1971.

Mause, Lloyd de, ed. *The History of Childhood*. New York: Harper, 1975.

Mazzacurati, G. *Forma e ideologia*. Naples: Liguori, 1974.

———. "Sui materiali in opera nelle *Piacevoli Notti* di Giovan Francesco Straparola" and "La Narrativa di Giovan Francesco Straparola: sociologia e structura del personaggio fiabesco." *Societe e strutture narrative dal Trecento al Cinquencento*. Naples: Liguori, 1971.

McKinley, Robin. *Deerskin*. New York: Ace Books, 1993.

Mead, Margaret, and Martha Wolfenstein, eds. *Childhood in Contemporary Cultures*. Chicago: University of Chicago Press, 1955.

Merritt, Russell, and J. B. Kaufman. *Walt in Wonderland: The Silent Films of Walt Disney*. Baltimore: Johns Hopkins University Press, 1993.

Miller, Alice. *The Drama of the Gifted Child*. Trans. Ruth Ward. New York: Basic Books, 1981.

———. *For Your Own Good: Hidden Cruelty in Child-Rearing and the Roots of Violence*. New York: Basic Books, 1983.

"Miss Piggy Went to Market and $150 Million Came Home." Interview with Jim Henson. *American Film* 15 (November 1989): 18–21.

Morrissey, Thomas J. "Alive and Well But Not Unscathed: A Response to Susan T. Gannon's *Pinocchio*: The First Hundred Years." *Children's Literature Association Quarterly* 7 (Summer 1982): 37–39.

Morrissey, Thomas J., and Richard Wunderlich. "Death and Rebirth in *Pinocchio*." *Children's Literature* 11 (1983): 64–75.

Mosley, Leonard. *Disney's World*. New York: Stein and Day, 1985.

Motte-Gillet, Anne, ed. *Conteurs italiens de la Renaissance*. Intr. Giancarlo Mazzacurati. Trans. Georges Kempf. Paris: Gallimard, 1993.

———. "Giovan Francesco Straparola: Les Facétieuses Nuits" in *Conteurs italiens de la Renaissance*. Ed. A. Motte-Gillet. Intr. Giancarlo Mazzacurati. Trans. Georges Kempf. Paris: Gallimard, 1993. 1386–1440.

Negt, Oskar, and Alexander Kluge. *Public Sphere and Experience: Toward an Analysis of the Bourgeois and Proletarian Public Sphere*. Intro. Miriam Hansen. Trans. Peter Labanyi, Jamie Owen Daniel, and Assenka Oksiloff. Minneapolis: University of Minnesota Press, 1993.

Oerella, Nicolas J. "An Essay on *Pinocchio*." *The Adventures of Pinocchio: Story of a Puppet*. Trans. Nicolas J. Perella. Berkeley: University of California Press, 1986. 1–69.

Perrault, Charles. *Contes*. Ed. Marc Soriano. Paris: Flammarion, 1989.

Pollock, Linda A. *Forgotten Children: Parent-Child Relations from 1500 to 1900*. Cambridge: Cambridge University Press, 1983.

Redford, Donald. "The Literary Motif of the Exposed Child." *Numen: International Review of the History of Religions* 14 (1967): 209–228.

Rodari, Gianni. "Pinocchio nella letteratura per l'infanzia." In *Studi Collodiani*. Pescia: Fondazione Nazionale Carlo Collodi, 1976. 37–57.

Rölleke, Heinz, ed. *Die älteste Märchensammlung der Brüder Grimm: Synopse der handschriftlichen Urfassung von 1810 und der Erstdruck von 1812*. Cologne-Genève: Fondation Martin Bodmer, 1975.

Rothman, Andrea. "The Henson Kids Carry On." *Business Week* 3198 (February 4, 1991): 72–73.

Rushdie, Salman. *Haroun and the Sea of Stories*. New York: Viking, 1990.

Schectman, Jacqueline. *The Stepmother in Fairy Tales: Bereavement and the Feminine Shadow*. Boston: Sigo Press, 1993.

Schenda, Rudolph. *Von Mund zu Ohr: Bausteine zu einer Kulturgeschichte volkstümlichen Erzählens in Europa.* Göttingen: Vandenhoeck and Ruprecht, 1993.

Schickel, Richard. *The Disney Version: The Life, Times, Art and Commerce of Walt Disney.* New York: Simon and Schuster, 1968.

Sendak, Maurice. "Walt Disney's Triumph: The Art of *Pinocchio.*" *Walt Disney's Version of Pinocchio.* New York: Abrams, 1989.

Shahar, Shulamith. *Childhood in the Middle Ages.* London: Routledge, 1990.

Smoodin, Eric Loren. *Animating Culture: Hollywood Cartoons from the Sound Era.* New Brunswick: Rutgers University Press, 1993.

———. ed. *Disney Discourse: Producing the Magic Kingdom.* New York: Routledge, 1994.

Solomon, Charles. *Enchanted Drawings: The History of Animation.* Avenel, N.J.: Wing Books, 1994.

Steinlein, Rüdiger. *Die domestizierte Phantasie: Studien zur Kinderliteratur, Kinderlektüre und Literaturpädagogik des 18. Jahrhunderts und frühen 19. Jahrhunderts.* Heidelberg: Carl Winter Universitätsverlag, 1987.

———. *Märchen als poetische Erziehungsform: Zum kinderliterarischen Status der Grimmschen "Kinder- und Hausmärchen."* Heft 29. Berlin: Humboldt-Universität, 1994.

Stephens, John Richard, ed. *The King of the Cats and Other Feline Fairy Tales.* London: Faber and Faber, 1993.

———. *The Enchanted Cat.* Rocklin, Calif.: Prima Publishing and Communications, 1990.

Stilson, Janet. "Mother Goose Rock 'n Rhyme." *TV Guide* 39 (January 12–18, 1991): 12.

———. "Shelley Duvall: The Fairy Godmother of Children's TV." *TV Guide* 39 (March 2–8, 1991): 23–27.

Stöber, August. *Volksbüchlein: Kinder- und Volksliedchen, Spielreime, Sprüche und Märchen.* Strasbourg: G. L. Schuler, 1842.

Straparola, Giovan Francesco. *Le Piacevoli Notti.* Ed. Pastore Stocchi. Rome-Bari: Laterza, 1975.

———. *The Facetious Nights of Straparola.* Trans. W. G. Waters.

Illustr. Jales Garnier and E. R. Hughes. 4 vols. London: Society of Bibliophiles, 1894.

Street, Douglas. "Pinocchio: From Picaro to Pipsqueak." In *Children's Novels and the Movies*, ed. Douglas Street. New York: Frederick Ungar, 1983.

Strinati, Dominic. *An Introduction to Theories of Popular Culture*. London: Routledge, 1995.

Teahan, James T. "Introduction." *The Pinocchio of C. Collodi*. Trans. James T. Teahan. New York: Schocken, 1985. xv–xxx.

———. "C. Collodi, 1826–1890." In *Writers for Children: Critical Studies of Major Authors Since the Seventeenth Century*. Ed. Jane M. Bingham. New York: Charles Scribner's Sons, 1988. 129–137.

Velde, Vivian Vande. *Tales from the Brothers Grimm and the Sisters Weird*. New York: Harcourt Brace, 1995.

Walker, Barbara G. *Feminist Fairy Tales*. San Francisco: Harper-Collins, 1996.

Warner, Marina. *From the Beast to the Blonde: On Fairytales and Their Tellers*. London: Chatto and Windus, 1994.

Weatherby, W. J. *Salman Rushdie: Sentenced to Death*. New York: Carroll and Graf, 1990.

Wette, Adelheid, and Engelbert Humperdinck. *Hänsel und Gretel*. Ed. Wolfram Humperdinck. Stuttgart: Reclam, 1952.

Woolery, George W. *Children's Television, the First Thirty-Five Years, 1946–1981*. Metuchen: Scarecrow Press, 1983–1985.

———. *Animated TV Specials: The Complete Directory to the First Twenty-Five Years, 1962–1987*. Metuchen: Scarecrow Press, 1989.

Wunderlich, Richard. *The Pinocchio Catalogue*. New York: Greenwood, 1988.

———. "De-Radicalizing *Pinocchio*." In *Functions of the Fantastic*. Ed. Joe Sanders. Westport: Greenwood, 1995. 19–28.

Wunderlich, Richard, and Thomas J. Morrissey. "The Desecration of *Pinocchio* in the United States." *The Horn Book Magazine* 58 (April 1982): 205–212.

———. "*Pinocchio* Before 1920: The Popular and the Pedagogical Traditions." *Italian Quarterly* 23 (Spring 1982): 61–72.

Zago, Ester. "Carlo Collodi as Translator: From Fairy Tale to Folk Tale." *Lion and Unicorn* 12 (1988): 61–73.

Zipes, Jack, ed. *Beauties, Beasts, and Enchantment: Classic French Fairy Tales.* New York: New American Library, 1989.

———. *Fairy Tale as Myth/Myth as Fairy Tale.* Lexington: University Press of Kentucky, 1994.

———. ed. *The Outspoken Princess and the Gentle Knight.* New York: Bantam, 1994.

Index